PRAISE FOR AND TOTO,

I found *And Toto, Too* enthralling: illuminating and wonderfully illustrative of how God gets to us, with shocks and disruptions, or blessings and calm, in all the seemingly ordinary "backyards" of our lives. Using the classic film *The Wizard of Oz* as a touch point throughout is fabulous — it's so familiar and works at such a charming, metaphorical level.

> Ron Hansen
> Best-selling author and Professor of Arts & Humanities at Santa Clara University
> San Jose, California

Nathan Castle's book exemplifies the work of the creative imagination at its best. How I wish that I had had this resource at hand during my long tenure as a University Chaplain — what a great book for discussion groups! Questioning minds and restive spirits will be drawn to this valuable resource that speaks to any generation - young or old.

> Raymond Judd Jr.
> Trinity University Chaplain, Emeritus

Nathan Castle helps us to see and discover our true self in the stories we read. He shares his insight into the spiritual truths within this classic film and opens us to a layer of meaning that can illuminate our own inner lives.

> Rev. Richard M. Kingsley
> Pastor, Corpus Christi Parish – Tucson, Arizona

A wonderfully accessible book that faces tough, real-life issues for college students head on — like trouble in school, problems with parents, addiction, and personal insecurity — filtered through the characters in *The Wizard of Oz*.

> Scotty McLennan
> Dean for Religious Life
> Memorial Church, Stanford University

PRAISE FOR AND TOTO, TOO

Father Nathan Castle plumbs the spiritual depths of the iconic film, illuminating the human quest for meaning and belonging with remarkable grace and accessibility. Readers will be immediately drawn in to his compelling tapestry of personal and mythic stories and be left with new insight, compassion and encouragement to live with authenticity and rapture.

Kerry A. Robinson

Executive Director of the National Leadership Roundtable on Church Management

Personal yet profound, filled with creative connections, *And Toto Too* is the kind of very readable book that can also change how you see everything! Nathan Castle knows how to write and also has something to say — when usually it is just one or the other.

Richard Rohr, O.F.M.

Best-selling author and Founder, Center for Action and Contemplation

Albuquerque, New Mexico

AND TOTO, TOO

AND TOTO, TOO:

AS A SPIRITUAL ADVENTURE

NATHAN G. CASTLE, O.P.

FIRST EDITION, JANUARY 2012

Copyright © 2011 by Good Dog Outreach

Published in the United States by Good Dog Outreach, Mt. Hood Parkdale, Oregon, 2012.

The Library of Congress has cataloged this edition as follows:

Castle, Nathan G., O.P., 1956, March 12 -
And Toto, Too: "The Wizard of Oz" as a Spiritual Adventure/by Nathan G. Castle, O.P. – 1st U.S. ed.

ISBN: 978-0-615-52474-0

© 2011 by Good Dog Outreach
All rights reserved. First edition 2012
Printed in the United States of America

Book cover and interior design by Doreen Hann
Dog cover photo by Joseph C. Dovala
Cathryn Castle Whitman and Gene Gentrup, editors.
Twelve/16 Design Group www.twelve16designgroup.com

Good Dog Outreach
6385 Dee Hwy.
Mt. Hood Parkdale, OR 97041
www.andtoto.org

DEDICATION

My sister Mimi reads all the time and lives in a house full of books. So when I had a draft of my book done I asked her to read it and give me some feedback. I was expecting grammatical corrections and more substantial suggested improvements. She said only two things, one a statement, the other a question: "I think it's a little jewel" and "Where is your mother?"

The jewel remark was kind, but the mom one was the most helpful. Dad plays a big role in *And Toto, Too*. He's in the prologue and is referenced throughout the book.

Mom's a no-show, it seems.

Except that, now that I think about it, she's all over it. She's on every page, and between every line. My mom, Miriam Castle, now over 90 and "young in heart," is the best person I've ever known. She's the most Christ-like. The most Toto-like. I hope you get to meet her someday.

I love you, Mom. I'm proud of you, too.

Nathan

Nathan G. Castle, O.P., is originally from Groves, Texas. He graduated from Trinity University in San Antonio and entered the Dominican order in 1979. Father Nathan received MA and MDiv degrees from the Dominican School of Philosophy and Theology at the Graduate Theological Union in Berkeley, California, and has served in campus ministries in California and Arizona for the last 22 years. He came to Stanford in 2007 and currently serves as pastor/director of the Catholic Community at Stanford. Father Nathan has chaired the executive board of the Catholic Campus Ministry Association (CCMA). He enjoys golf, spending time with friends and cheering on his favorite sports teams, especially Stanford football and Houston Astros baseball.

"Late have I loved you,
O Beauty ever ancient and ever new!
Late have I loved you!
And, behold, you were within me,
and I out of myself,
and there I searched for you."

– SAINT AUGUSTINE

Confessions, X, 27, translated in *Theology and Discovery:
Essays in Honor of Karl Rahner, S.J.* (1980) edited by William J. Kelly

(Sero te amavi, pulchritudo tam antique et tam nova, sero te amavi!
et ecce intus eras et ego foris, et ibi te quaerebam.)

THANKS & PRAISE

"Curseit! Curseit" Somebody always helps that girl."

— THE WICKED WITCH OF THE WEST

It's true. Dorothy got lots of help from loyal friends and folks she'd just met, human, magical, canine, feline. She was helped by both those seen and unseen. Me, too.

In fact, I want to say thanks in advance to those who'll be helping in the months and years ahead.

But for now… thanks to my Dominican brothers, especially for the sabbatical time back in 2006 and 2007 when the first chapters of *And Toto, Too* came to be.

Thanks to Cathryn, my sister/publisher/publicist/friend and founding member of the Twelve/16 Design Group. You and Doreen and Gene and Jim and Joe got my message from unseen to seen.

Thanks to my family and all the friends and students who read chapters early on and added helpful advice, and to Dr. Richard R. Rutter of the International Wizard of Oz Club.

Thanks to my Internet friends, George Leaman, who found the Augustine quote for me, and to the people of Wikipedia and the Online Etymology Dictionary.

Often I've prayed in the Spirit with the whole cast and crew of *The Wizard of Oz*. Thanks to all of you who left a bit of yourself for us all to enjoy. I didn't always know exactly who to thank, but know that you're in the credits scrolling in my heart.

Matt and Beloved Barbara, Beautiful Betty, Frank and Maud, Judy and Vinny, Bert and Louis… you're the best. Michael and P.J., Messenger and Dominic and Kinsman Paul, I can't thank you enough. And Marcus, thanks for loving my baby sister.

Thanks to Buddy the Dog-Faced Boy, Sandy, Ginger, Toots, Linus, Holt, Jonah, and Toto for helping me recognize God's loving canine face.

Thanks to my communities in Menlo Park and at Stanford. Billygene, thanks for saying yes to living with me three times over the years. Isaiah, Nancy, Teresa, Lourdes, Ramona, M'Lis, Guillermo and Iris, thanks for doing more than your share to enable me to do this book thing.

And finally, Richard, like Dorothy said to Scarecrow and Tin Man, "You're the best friend anybody ever had."

Friend of My Heart, thanks for creating and loving me and all of the above.

TABLE OF CONTENTS

TABLE OF CONTENTS

TABLE OF CONTENTS

How I Ran Away
Without Going
Anywhere

There weren't VCRs yet.

Or DVDs or TiVo. There wasn't cable or satellite or YouTube, or downloads or apps. You couldn't watch a movie on your phone either. Later those dreams people dared to dream really did come true.

But we weren't a modern Stone Age family either, just kids growing up in the early '60s. The antenna on our roof pulled in three channels; two clear, one fuzzy. In our big family we'd sometimes fight over who got to pick what show we'd watch. But not when *The Wizard of Oz* was on.

Everybody wanted to watch that, and it only came on once a year. It was an event nobody wanted to miss. And I don't mean just kids. Grown-ups watched, too. The neighbors came over. We made popcorn. Watching *The Wizard of Oz* together was a big deal. I wondered why even then.

Television united people when President Kennedy was killed, and again when men first walked on the moon. But that was different. *The Wizard of Oz* was just an old movie. Still, the story seemed to have a hold on people young and old.

The story of my early years now seems unremarkable enough. I was the middle of five kids in a stable Catholic home. I was never hungry, beaten or abused. When I look around and see how many children have such a difficult start in life I can only be thankful that I had it so good. Nevertheless everybody has a story, and I'm no exception.

My world was our busy family and my little Catholic school. I was a quiet, shy kid growing up in the traffic of our household, content not to be the center of attention. In fact, a lot of the time I preferred to be unnoticed. I was a good student. In our little school I'd compete for whatever honors there were: membership in the smart-kid reading group, the most stars next to my name. On report card day our family had a custom of getting dressed up and eating dinner at a Mexican restaurant, El Patio. The dinner would honor the person with the best report card. This was a big deal in my little world, my moment in the sun. Often enough I was an honoree on report card day and earned the acknowledgement of my dad. He was a mystery to me. I didn't really know how to talk with him and was kind of afraid of him. In a big family it was easy enough for each of us to go about our business interacting only on occasion. Report card day was an occasion.

Ours was a K-through-8 Catholic school. I went through kindergarten and grades 1-7 with most of the same kids. Eighth-graders were the leaders, of course, and got to do all of the cool stuff. Because our school had no public address system, eighth-graders acted as couriers, carrying messages from the principal's office to the various classrooms. One late afternoon on a Friday in late April of my seventh-grade year, an eighth-grade girl came to our classroom with an announcement for the teacher to read. It was a thunderclap out of the blue. *On Monday, people will be here from the public schools to receive your transcripts and to register you for classes for next year. Our school will close at the end of May.*

So that was that.

There went my little world. It just dried up and blew away. I went from a class of 17 to a new school of 900. They were 900 of the most foul-mouthed kids I'd ever been around. They were angry all the time and always shouting this angry phrase: *Fork you! FORK YOU!* I had no idea what silverware had to do with being so angry. I just hid in the library and tried to stay out of the way. I was kind of a jock at my old school. People wanted me on their team. Not at the new school. There was a compulsory gym class, the kind with lockers and group showers. I wasn't good at much of anything, mostly because, at 13, my growth spurt was coming later than it did for most guys. That was painfully obvious to any onlooker in the locker room.

One day all my frustration came together into a kind of adolescent "perfect storm." At the center of it was a rope dangling from the rafters of the gym.

One by one the other guys in the class scampered up the rope like squirrels. Some struggled a bit, the coaches shouting at them to keep trying. I failed badly at my first attempt, making my way to the back of the line. Eventually everyone had made it to the top of the gym and back down. Everybody but me. I tried again, the only one of 50 guys unable to do the stupid thing. One of the coaches got beneath me and tried to push me up, because that would make it so much easier. It only made me look like a worse loser to the rest of the class. When it was clear to everyone that I was hopeless, the coach shouted, "All right everybody, hit the showers!"

Report card day rolled around the following week. At my old school all the grades were written on one card. It was different at my new school. Here they gave you six different cards, one for each subject. Six A's would put me on the Honor Roll.

I walked home from school that afternoon and turned into our yard. There was Dad, sweeping the porch.

"Report card day, idinit?"

"Yessir."

"Well lemme see um."

XXVI

He flipped through the first five cards, all A's. When he got to the sixth one all he said was, "What happened in P.E.?"

I split in two. On the outside I replied, "I couldn't climb a rope." Inside I screamed, "*FORK YOU!*"

As quickly as I could I went to my room, closed the door, and sat on the edge of the bed, shaking. Tears rolled down the inside of my cheeks, because big boys don't cry.

At least not on the outside.

I sat there on the edge of my bed and concluded that my life sucked and nobody gave a damn about me. I decided I needed to run away, without going anywhere. And so I needed a plan. It was a given in our family that all of us would go off to college. But that was still almost five years away. What was I supposed to do in the meantime? I could at least go to the Catholic high school for grades nine through 12. But I still had to live with my family and, hardest of all, with my dad.

Here's the plan I came up with that day: Be perfect. I figured if I was perfectly obedient and responsible beyond my years, I wouldn't need parenting. I'd raise myself. My parents had four other kids to raise anyway. I wanted to be perfect, not so that I'd be noticed, but so that I'd be invisible. If I could just do that for the next four and a half years, I could make my escape, and go find some other place to live. That was my plan.

It turned out to be a pretty good plan. I went to a small Catholic high school for grades 9 through 12. I got good grades. I stayed out of trouble. In my senior year I was elected student body president. At home I tried not to be too obvious about saying little or nothing to my dad. Lots of teenagers don't say much to their parents, right?

In the spring of my senior year of high school it was time to pick a college. I'd done my homework and made my decision — a college about a five-hour drive away. It was among the most expensive private colleges in the state. I'd earned a partial scholarship, but this would still be at my parents' expense. They were pleased. I was pleased. That was settled. It was now March. By August I'd be on my way.

Back at school one of my friends, Brenda Carona, was all excited about an experience she'd had and wanted everyone to know about. She'd been on a retreat weekend at the Newman Center at the local college. This was a Catholic campus ministry center for the college students. They'd had a retreat weekend that the college students organized for high school seniors. She said it was "life-changing," which I thought was OK if you wanted to have your life changed. It didn't interest me and I declined her invitation to go on the next one. Brenda pleaded. I told her I wouldn't know anybody there.

But she persisted. She recruited just about everyone I knew. My I-won't-know-anybody excuse wouldn't hold up. I knew my reluctance was really based in fear and I've never liked the way I feel when I make fear-based decisions. So, I relented and went on a retreat.

I've been a Catholic all my life and figure I know how to do what Catholics do. There must be about 60 kids gathered for this thing. They organize us into groups of about seven or eight and refer to us as "families." Each family is led by a couple of college students. I'm acquainted with two of the people in my group. The rest are strangers. Since this is a church thing I'm expecting it to be about command-ments and sacraments and prayers. But the first thing they ask us is, "What do you think about your parents?" I'm completely surprised. We'd gone to church every Sunday of my life, but I'd never really seen faith and family life mix.

One by one the members of my "family" start to open their hearts and speak intimately about their home life. Some of their stories are full of painful struggles. I'm amazed that such ordinary-looking people have such extraordinary depth. We seldom spoke about our feelings in my household; I didn't know anyone ever did. I marvel at the respect and reverence we have for each other as we listen to and support one another. At school we had mandatory church services from time to time but there seemed to be a kind of code that required a bored aloofness. Here some of the same people are quite obviously fully engaged in the retreat. When it's my turn to offer my story, I decide to take the risk and tell the truth.

The truth is, now that my time at home is short, I'm feeling rotten about my relationship with my dad. I know that his hard work will be bankrolling my es-cape from his household. I don't like what that says about me, and I tell these kind people so. It seems like I ought to try to talk with him from the heart at least once before leaving home. It seems like an unrepeatable moment in life that calls for some honesty. But how would I find the words and the nerve to talk to the man?

XXIX

AND TOTO, TOO

The retreat winds down on Sunday afternoon and ends with a Mass. I'd done that hundreds of times before, even daily when I was in elementary school. So, we take our places sitting on the floor in this informal but powerful gathering. Near the end it's time for Communion. I'd received Communion since the first grade. I couldn't know how different that was about to be with my newly opened heart.

I go forward and put the Communion wafer in my mouth. Our belief is that we're receiving the fullness of God into ourselves in the Body of Christ. I'd had no problem believing that. I never had. This time, though, I was in for a surprise.

As I return to my place my whole body begins to pulse and throb. Every cell in my body is vibrating and heating up and I'm full of love. I know it's the Lord and my body is responding to Him. I start thinking of Bible stories of people having ecstatic religious experiences and here I am having one of my own! I'm a pretty strong introvert, so I'm not jumping around or rolling on the floor. But inside I'm

XXX

having my own private Pentecost. I get back to my place, close my eyes and sit down on the floor, with people all around me … and I start to cry. This time the tears are on the outside of my face. Now I'm figuring everyone must be staring at me wondering what's going on. So I peer out, expecting to find everyone staring, only to find that no one is looking at me at all. I learn in that moment that when you think it's all about you, it usually isn't.

So, I go home, back to my bedroom. Down the hall is Dad, asleep. He works very erratic hours, day and night, and sleeps whenever he can. One of the cardinal rules of our household is, *Don't wake up Daddy!* Nevertheless, I know I need to talk to him, and that if I don't do it quickly I might lose my nerve. On the edge of my bed I say a prayer. As I do, my body quakes and the palms of my hands pulse and get hot as they did at the Mass on the retreat earlier. Whatever this new thing is, it isn't confined to an emotional moment on a retreat. It has come home with me. The love and the power of God have followed me home.

I start down the hall, then falter and dart back into my room. But I have to get this done. So I make my way to his room and, with difficulty, wake up Daddy. Here's the short version: I ask him if he knew I'd stopped talking to him years ago. He said, "Yup. I just didn't know what to do about it." I get a few things off my chest, tell him I love him, and feel a huge release. Near the time of his death 23 years later, he said to me, "Whatever you did that day, do more of it. It really matters."

One week after the retreat there's a "retreat reunion." I return to the place and the people who have changed my life. I'd felt a sense of lightness, freedom and joy all week long. I feel like I'm starting my life over. The leaders gather everyone into a big circle and ask this question: "Does anyone feel any different than they did last week?" I think to myself, "Well, for cryin' out loud, I feel completely different! But the basics of my life are still the same. How can I put this experience into words?"

And then it comes to me. I don't wait my turn. I raise my hand and speak my truth. I'm an 18-year-old guy who, at the moment, feels like a little girl in a children's movie. "I feel like Dorothy, Dorothy in *The Wizard of Oz*. I haven't really gone anywhere, but I feel like I've been on a journey everywhere and back again. And there really is no place like home."

That's all 37 years ago, now. And it's still the most important thing that's ever happened to me. I learned to live in my own skin, to be fully present to all of the moments and persons and events of my own life. I also learned I wasn't alone in here. God who created me and had built himself into me was my constant companion. This simple and complex story needed to be told, and at the moment I was asked to tell it I found my voice by using the language of a children's movie. I have paid attention to *The Wizard of Oz* ever since. Almost daily, most times before noon, I hear or see a reference to it in a conversation, in an advertisement, on the radio, somewhere. This story and its characters are well-embedded in our culture and in our imaginations. I think I have something to say about it. For years I have been threatening to write a book about it. And now I have. I hope you enjoy it.

CHAPTER 1

In the Beginning:
L. Frank Baum

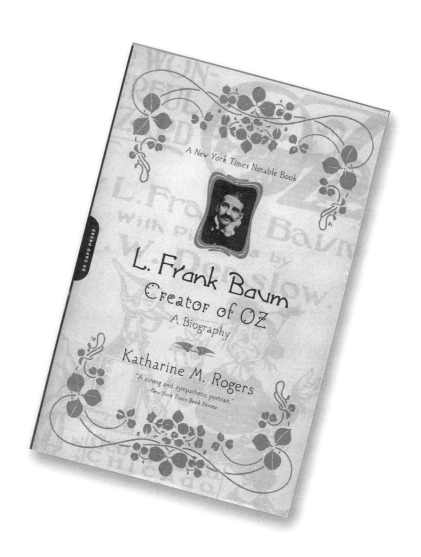

A New York Times Notable Book

L. Frank Baum
Creator of OZ
A Biography

Katharine M. Rogers

"A strong and sympathetic portrait."
—New York Times Book Review

Everything that is created
exists first in the mind of its creator.

Oz and all who live or visit there enter the heart of L. Frank Baum. Because of the influence that *The Wizard of Oz* has had on my life, I've done what is within my power to get to know Frank Baum.

When I want to get to know someone who has written or is written about, I read. Two biographies of Baum are readily available: *L. Frank Baum: Creator of Oz* by Katharine M. Rogers gives the reader the benefit of the most recent scholarship regarding Baum's life. Baum's son, Frank Joslyn Baum, wrote *To Please a Child: A Biography of L. Frank Baum, Royal Historian of Oz*, in 1961. It has a natural intimacy about it, as the author shares childhood memories of his father as husband, father and storyteller. Both books help give the reader a sense of who Frank Baum was as a person.

There's another thing I do. I pray. I'm convinced of two things: We all survive our deaths, and heaven isn't far away.

When I've tried to get to know, and even to befriend Frank Baum, I just say a prayer. I imagine what I call the Holy Spirit, which just means

3

"sacred breath," being inside my body. I go to the Internet of my imagination and type in "L. Frank Baum." I don't know how prayer or Internet search engines work, I just know that they do. I don't presume distance; I presume presence. Jesus said, "The Kingdom of God is in your midst." So when I've read about Frank Baum, I've asked him to look over my shoulder or get in my imagination and help me get to know him. I also promise not to believe everything I read. The most important thing I can say about Frank Baum is that I consider him my friend.

All of us are complex. Describing anyone is a big job, one that should be approached humbly. But we describe people all the time, don't we? What follows is my attempt to say a few things that I think are important to know about Frank Baum. I'll speak about him in the past tense, because I'm thinking of aspects of his experiences that I believe shaped and came to characterize him.

Frank was a loved person who knew he was loved. He was born to parents who welcomed him into their family. He went on to become a loving person who welcomed a wife and children into his life. What an advantage it is in life to know oneself to be loved.

I think Frank learned early on that people are more important than things. His family enjoyed newly acquired wealth, and he lacked for nothing. He wasn't spoiled, but his parents spent their money on what they valued. Frank was valued. He had good tutors; he learned about the power of ideas and enjoyed the support of his parents when he had an idea that captured his imagination. When he showed an interest in writing as a child, his parents bought him a printing press. Later, when he became a young playwright and aspiring actor, his parents invested in a theater.

Another person might have grown to prize material wealth. Interestingly, while many children's stories feature the search for buried treasures, there is no pot of gold at the end of any rainbow Frank Baum wrote about. Anything worth pursuing had value greater than money. Frank used money as a resource. That's an interesting word, *resource*. It involves the idea of returning to the source, the beginning. Even in the seasons of his life when Frank made significant money, he turned right around and plowed it into the next excellent idea. His beloved wife, Maud, learned early on to keep a close eye on the family finances. Frank could live with money or without it, but Maud and their four sons could not. Frank was happy to have Maud take care of their financial matters, leaving him free to focus on his latest "project of the moment."

Well-loved people are often the best risk takers. Knowing that you'll be loved even in failure can take the fear out of going for broke. Baum was broke more than once. The Baums even had to declare bankruptcy in the last decade of his life. But he could move to the Dakota Territory and open a lavish bazaar in Aberdeen, or build one of the first homes in Hollywood and open his own movie studio. He could take his mother-in-law's advice and write stories for children, fully expecting that they'd be published. Sometimes the risks panned out. Other times they didn't. No one ever accused Frank Baum of playing it safe.

Well-loved people often become good lovers. Frank's marriage was a lifelong love affair. Both of his biographies recount tender stories of the bond forged between Frank and Maud. Though they were, at heart, private people, their home was open to a wide circle of friends. The neighborhood children knew when Frank was at home during his years as an often-absent traveling salesman. He read his stories not only to his own four sons, but also to all their friends. Their Wisconsin vacation home teemed with life. On Coronado Island, near San Diego, there were golf companions and card partners. In the last decade of his life, in Hollywood, there was the Lofty and Exalted Order of Uplifters — a gang of fun-loving companions who staged musical follies and shared laughs. People loved to be around Frank Baum. He had more than enough love to share.

I love the word *philanthropist*. It means a lover of people. Philanthropists give what they have to others, whose lives are enriched by the gifts. Any artist can toil away at mere self-expression. Baum wasn't just a writer; he was a communicator. To commune or to create communion means to be "one with" another. Baum would write a book, a play or a screenplay with his audience in mind, especially the children. "… To please a child is a sweet and lovely thing that warms one's heart and brings its own rewards," he said. (*To Please A Child*; Frank Joslyn Baum and Russell P. MacFall, Reilly & Lee Co., 1961) He often collaborated with others who took his original ideas and recast them. He seemed to give birth to his characters and stories and allow others to step into the middle of his creations and change them all around. His stories were adapted for the stage during his lifetime, sometimes bearing only scant resemblance to his original version. The 1939 MGM screenplay of *The Wizard of Oz*, written 20 years after his passing, is significantly different from the book he wrote. The recent success of the book and play *Wicked* continues a creative process put in motion by Baum. He was happy to create something beautiful and equally happy to have others improve upon it.

One expression of Frank Baum's love of people was his interest in one of the most controversial political issues of his day: women's suffrage. His mother-in-law, Matilda Joslyn Gage, was a well-known advocate of women's rights. He worked with her, and with Maud early in their marriage while living in the Dakota Territories, on securing the right for women to vote. His children's stories often feature strong, compassionate heroines, like Dorothy. She and his other female protagonists do not pine away hoping to be rescued by a Prince Charming. They use their own resourcefulness and the gifts of their companions to solve their problems. Often church people take up the cause of the weak. But sometimes they don't. Baum heard one too many sermons opposing women's suffrage, or claiming that God had designed women to be the weaker sex. Consequently he was a less than avid churchgoer.

Many of Baum's stories draw upon the journey motif. He seemed to look at life as a journey. His own life found him journeying and creating temporary homes across the continent. "Home" was not just one's place of origin, but rather the place of one's current rootedness. Frank and Maud could transplant themselves and be at home wherever they went. Loved people can do that with ease. Dorothy is still learning to do that when we first meet her. But she learns, as I think Baum did, that there is a deeper sense of home than Kansas or any one place on earth can provide. Frank Baum, as a loved person, was at home in his own skin. He knew that being at home in yourself was indeed the rainbow's end.

CHAPTER 2

Looking
Inside

"The lesson of The Wizard of Oz is, well, when you think you're lacking something, where do you find it? You look inside!"

– HARRISON ELLENSHAW, VISUAL EFFECTS DESIGNER
WARNER BROTHERS THREE-DISC COLLECTOR'S EDITION, DISC TWO
"THE ART OF THE IMAGINATION: A TRIBUTE TO OZ"

Frank Baum wasn't afraid of being corny.

So *The Wizard of Oz* has a moral. It's a simple universal truth a child is capable of understanding. You could try to dress it up with more complex adult vocabulary, but a simple truth is best spoken simply. Jesus once addressed religious scholars and reminded them that unless they had the heart of a child they couldn't enter the Kingdom of Heaven.

When Dorothy stands ready to return home, she's asked to reflect upon her experience. "What have you learned, Dorothy?" The Tin Man asks. She replies that if she ever goes looking for her heart's desire again, "I won't look any further than my own backyard." Her "own backyard" is not a patch of dirt on a Kansas farm.

It's herself. She belongs everywhere because she can now dwell in her own skin. She's home already, even before she clicks her heels together.

Earlier in her journey, when she was lost and clearly couldn't go back the way she came, she acknowledged that she was powerless. There in Munchkinland she seems to have gotten some bum advice. Glinda the Good Witch suggests, *"The only person who might know would be the great and wonderful Wizard of Oz himself."* Was Glinda taken in by this humbug, too? But here's the worst part: *"He lives in the Emerald City and that's a long journey from here. Did you bring your broomstick with you?"*

The bad news is that there's someone with the power to help you but he doesn't live here and you'll have to go God knows where to get to him. That bad news has been handed down for eons. And often the people delivering that message seem to be in charge.

Where God is concerned, people have long been taught that God lives somewhere else. A particular nation, a certain mountaintop, the sky, outer space, some other dimension where maybe you'll get to go after you die — and then only if you stay on God's good side and don't screw up your life. Even the best of the world's religious traditions have some of this stuff going on within them. But most also have a deeper message: God lives everywhere, including here, or herein.

Because I know the Judeo-Christian tradition best, that's where I'm most competent to speak. Because I'm a Christian and a Catholic priest this will be the "home turf" from which I venture out to comment upon the wonderful *Wizard of Oz.*

In my line of work I do a fair amount of pastoral counseling. I listen. I think a lot of people believe in God, or at least they want to. I don't mind being God's instrument, but I don't want to be God's surrogate. God will do his own listening, given the chance. I remind them that if God is everywhere, and they're somewhere, then God and they overlap. If that's true, then God isn't just above or around them, but also exists within them. So how do you start a prayer? Our Father who art in heaven? Or, hello in there? I think they both work.

Frank Baum was raised a Christian and was well-acquainted with the Hebrew Scriptures and the New Testament. Auntie Em, in a moment of exasperation at Miss Gulch — which the screenplay notes call "an expression of repressed anger" — says, "For 23 years I've been dying to tell you what I thought of you … and now … being a Christian woman — I can't say it!" Clearly, *The Wizard of Oz* is not a religious book or movie but the story develops themes that one can also find in spiritual writings. Baum knew the Jewish and Christian scriptures well. So do I. And I think Baum recast some of these themes to great effect in *The Wizard of Oz*. I'd like to explore this idea in the next chapter. ❧

CHAPTER 3

Uncommon
Common Journeys

The Book of Exodus, the second

book of the Bible, begins with a whole group of people who are unhappy where they are and long to be somewhere else. That's because they've been hauled off into slavery. They dream of going home.

A baby is born in this foreign land, Egypt. His name is Moses. We no sooner meet him in the story, when a powerful person with the law on his side wants to kill the little baby. In fact, this guy is the king, and he orders all the Hebrew baby boys killed. "Throw into the river every boy that is born to the Hebrews," Pharaoh says. Someone who loves little Moses, his mother, with the help of some friends, creates a plan to save his life. They put him in a basket, place it in the river, and he floats to safety.

He'll grow up quickly, as characters do in stories. One minute he's a baby, but in the next paragraph he's all grown up. He's tending flocks when he sees this odd burning bush. A heavenly voice says, "I need you to bring my suffering people out of slavery and lead them on a journey. I will be with you." And Moses says, "And who would you be? What's your name?" The voice replies, "I AM." And off they go, gathering traveling companions along the way. There are many hardships, betrayals and misadventures. They forge bonds of community and come to understand themselves. Eventually they arrive again at their original home.

In the first book of the New Testament, The Gospel of Matthew, the story line begins with another newborn child. A voice from heaven says, "His name will be I AM WITH YOU." At birth he's placed in a manger — an animal's food box — for temporary safekeeping. But it's not safe there! A king wants this child dead,

AND TOTO, TOO

too! Jesus, as he is known, is taken on a journey by the parents who love him. They run away to a place where there isn't any trouble — Egypt. He's there for a few years, and is an adult a chapter later. That won't be the last of his travels.

And then there's this other book. By now you know the one. There's this little guy, Toto. His name means totality, everything. (It reminds me of Jesus. At the start of the last book of the Bible, the Book of Revelation, he says, "I AM the alpha and the omega, the beginning and the end.")[1] Dorothy (her name means "gift of God") loves little Toto, but someone's trying to kill him! This mean old woman named Gulch who owns half the county wants him dead. She's got a legal document allowing her to take the dog. *"Here's what I'm taking him in,"* she sneers. She produces a picnic basket — yet another food container put to an odd use. But he'll escape and run back home. Later, after Miss Gulch morphs into The Wicked Witch of the West, Toto will encounter her again, this time in the tower room of her dark castle. Angry at being denied the powerful ruby slippers, she shrieks, "Throw that basket into the river and drown him!" The screenplay notes read: "CLOSE SHOT—BASKET. TOTO suddenly pushes his head out and scrambles out and across the floor and out the door." Dorothy cries, *"Run, Toto, run!"* And the journey continues. Incidentally, have you ever noticed the only prop Judy Garland carries down the Yellow Brick Road? It's a basket.

1. Revelation 1:8

On one of the DVDs in the 2005 Turner Entertainment Co. Three-Disc Collector's Edition of *The Wizard of Oz*, Angela Lansbury claims that the 1939 MGM version of the story has been seen by more people than any movie ever made. I don't know where Angela gets her information, but she's never lied to me before. So if she's right and this is the most widely seen movie ever made, I want to ask, *Why?* What is it about this story that touches people so deeply?

I am a preacher; the point of preaching is to communicate good news to people. To do that, one first has to gain their attention, and with God's help one hopes to be invited into their hearts. I pay attention to anything that people take to heart. So many people have invited this story and these characters into their hearts. I want to know why.

Because you have read this far I can safely assume you have some interest in this story, too. In Munchkinland, once Dorothy has decided to launch out on her journey, she is encouraged musically, over and over, to:

"Follow the Yellow Brick Road.
Follow the Yellow Brick Road.
Follow, follow, follow, follow,
Follow the Yellow Brick Road."

She does so, but barely makes it beyond the gates of Munchkinland before the road forks off in three directions. I used to think it was critical that she pick the right unmarked path. But will only one of her possible choices take her where she wants to go? Maybe whichever path she chooses will lead to the Emerald City. She might meet different companions with different backgrounds, interests and desires.

Faced with this dilemma, Dorothy asks *(herself? Toto? God? the universe?)*, *"Now which way do we go?"* A brainless direction-giver points the way. Or ways. *"Pardon me. That way is a very nice way. It's pleasant down that way, too."* And, pointing in both directions, The Scarecrow concludes, *"Of course, people do go both ways!"*

In the end, Dorothy must choose her own way. Everyone must. Then she's free to invite others along. They needn't be looking for the same things to share the common journey and to help each other along the way. They needn't even be whole. They can hobble along if that's the best they can do. The Scarecrow falters; Dorothy steadies him. And together, as the song says, they're …

"… off to see the Wizard,
The Wonderful
Wizard of Oz."

So at this point, I must ask you: Would you like to come along with me? Would you feel degraded to be seen in the company of a cowardly Catholic priest? We can be frightening. Does mention of the name

Jesus creep you out? Some people want nothing to do with his followers, and they have their reasons.

And then there's the whole "God" thing. Upon arriving at the Emerald City, Oz's doorman, shocked at the travelers' request, stammers, *"Oh — oh — the Wizard? Ah — but nobody can see the Great Oz! Nobody's ever seen the Great Oz! Even I've never seen him!"* Dorothy asks, guilelessly, *"Well, then, how do you know there is one?"* Maybe you're agnostic or an atheist, or too disinterested in religious matters to even accept either of those labels. Just so you know, you're still welcome to be my companion and fellow traveler.

How do you feel about self-reflection? Travelers do have to be willing to examine their lives, to take stock of themselves honestly, and to ask for what they need. Are you living an examined life? Are you willing to try?

Finally, do you like the movie? In the following chapters I'm planning to go through the film scene by scene and comment about them. I'll be using the DVD I mentioned earlier. It would be handy to have a copy of it to watch as we go along. So, are you with me?

Then, to Oz?

To Oz!

CHAPTER 4

The Characters

From now on, all of my references to the story will be from the screenplay[1] and the 1939 MGM film. Though the book is a classic it is the movie that is better-known. Both the book and the screenplay use a familiar literary structure of prologue, main body of the story, and an epilogue. In the film conflict arises in black-and-white Kansas, develops throughout the colorful journey through Oz, and is resolved in the "no place like home" Kansas epilogue.

Matthew's gospel contains a prologue, chapters 1 and 2, in which we meet the child, Jesus, who immediately runs afoul of powerful, cruel forces. Then, the next 23 chapters feature the collecting of a group of companions who join him along a linearly driven plot line featuring a road leading to a city of destiny. Mark's gospel, from which Matthew borrows freely, makes the road or "way" motif even more explicit. I don't know whether Baum was following the gospels' lead. This structure provides the framework for an unfolding drama.

In *The Wizard of Oz*, we meet almost all of the story's major characters, or at least a foreshadowing of who they will become, while still in Kansas.

First there's Dorothy. She's this archetypical farm girl. In Greek, *"Doro"* means gift; *"theos"* is God, from which our English word, *"theology"* derives. So, Dorothy is a gift from God walking around on the Earth. I think Frank Baum did that on purpose. I think he wanted children, young and old, to think of themselves as a gift from God to others and of their own lives as a gift.

[1] The Wizard of Oz: The Screenplay; Noel Langley, Florence Ryerson, and Edgar Allan Woolf, Delta, 1989

We know little about Dorothy's background, except that she's being raised, not by her parents, but by an aunt and uncle. And they appear to have no other children. There must be a sad story there, but we don't know it. Has she been orphaned? Has she living parents who are incapable of raising her? We don't know and we aren't told. Much of life is like that. We're surrounded daily by familiar faces we barely know, some of them in our own households.

We learn that she is a loving child and a loyal friend. She is not easily frightened, nor is she accepting of an unjust status quo. Suffering makes one either bitter or compassionate; Dorothy has chosen compassion.

Toto is a dog. Dogs are known as man's best friend. In Dorothy's life, Toto is love incarnate. He is with her always, in Kansas, Oz and Kansas. She treasures him and holds him close to her heart. His name means "completeness." Nothing can contain

him: Put him in a basket and he escapes. Locked rooms pose no problems. He runs to get help to save his beloved. He reveals the proud humbug behind the curtain, and prevents one last false promise from dissolving into thin air when he leaps out of the carnival balloon at the last minute, prompting Dorothy to follow.

As I mentioned earlier, in the last book of the Bible, Jesus is referred to as the Alpha and the Omega, the beginning, the end, and everything in between. He is Totality. Toto, I believe, is a Christ figure in *The Wizard of Oz*. Is that too much of a stretch for you? I can only ask you to try to have the heart of a child.

Aunt Em, she's an archetype of the harried, overworked woman whose life is hard. She's described as "careworn." She's earned every one of those wrinkles loving and serving those around her. True, she's indelicate, but women like Em are busy running the world! When we first meet her, Dorothy is breathlessly agitated about Miss Gulch attacking Toto. What's Em doing that makes it impossible for her to listen? She's saving lives. The incubator's broken and she and Henry are counting chicks as she cradles them in her apron and pulls them to her breast. She ends her count at 70, a biblical number of completeness. She's completely absorbed in her work, and inattentive at the time to Dorothy. Have you ever been in either of their positions, ignoring a loved one while tending to pressing business, or being ignored by the one you love at the moment that you rely upon their support? Most of us can relate.

A little later Em is threatening to fire "three shiftless farmhands" and, after they're back to work, offering them a snack: crullers she's just fried. Later, when Dorothy is called to reflect, she'll remember that *"I had the measles once ... and she stayed by me every minute!"* So, Em might not be perfect, but she tries hard. Were you raised by parents who were flawed but who tried hard? Or who were just flawed in ways that hurt you?

Miss Almira Gulch; she's an archetype, too. She's a dry riverbed, unattractive inside and out. Toto is considered an intruder in *her* garden. She might own half the county but has no joy and certainly no compassion. Do you remember the story of an earthly garden where someone grabbed so she could be "like the gods, having all knowledge"? Nothing's ever enough. Miss Gulch is always empty. She's got the law on her side, too; the powerful often use the law to dominate others. One wonders if she ever felt loved. As the story unfolds, she'll morph into The Wicked Witch of the West. As we meet her, all we know of her is that she's just suffered the sudden, violent death of her sister. The book and the play *Wicked* explore her background. Everybody has a story. We're all brothers and sisters. But sometimes all we see in front of us is someone who'd like to hurt us. And, for now, that's Miss Gulch.

Uncle Henry: He's almost not there at all. He's a very minor character. It's clear Aunt Em rules this roost. That's not surprising, given Frank Baum's penchant for heroines, succeeding against all odds through their pluck and ingenuity. Henry has a bemused sense of humor, but is more of an observer of the events around him than a shaper of them.

The farmhands, Hunk, Hickory and Zeke, in the Kansas scenes foreshadow traits that will define their Oz counterparts. Watch carefully to notice how. Hunk, who will become The Scarecrow, accuses Dorothy of having no brains at all. Hickory, in a scene in the screenplay but deleted from the final cut of the film, accuses Miss Gulch of being heartless and tells Dorothy, *"You know, you should have a little more heart yourself, and have pity on her.*" And Zeke, shaken by Dorothy's tumble into the pigsty, is accused of letting, "*a little old pig make a coward of ya.*"

Professor Marvel is an interesting guy. We meet him in a ditch (gulch?) with only a trickle of water. He's alongside Dorothy's road to nowhere/anywhere. Remember, the story was written in 1900 at the end of one era and the beginning of another. He's old; she's young. He exemplifies the 19th-century American archetype for flight: running away to join the circus! He ends up all alone, with only his horse to talk to. Here are some of his traits: He's a humbug, but not a bad man. He's compassionate and good-humored. Wisdom, for him, is accessed by "*reaching out into the infinite*" like the priests of the gods Isis and Osiris. He doesn't know the God of Moses who is I AM WITH YOU. Later he'll allow others to think of him as a distant mystical power. He gets Dorothy to return home by rethinking, by reflecting on her experiences. Watch how he does that in the film. He cares about her journey and helps her choose to return home.

Now that we've met the characters, let's see them in action. Let's start the movie.

CHAPTER 5

Watching the Movie

" It's always best to start at the beginning..."

- GLINDA, TO DOROTHY IN MUNCHKINLAND

The preamble to the film is a dedication.

It speaks in terms of faithful service to the Young in Heart. The story itself is personified. The reader/viewer who has been faithful to it in return is the honoree. There is then, a relationship acknowledged between the story and the viewer.

Photos and posters from *The Wizard of Oz* are everywhere. Stills of the four principal characters on the Yellow Brick Road are commonplace, as are Munchkinland scenes, and the scene of the Emerald City glistening in the distance, the poppy field carpeting the foreground. The very first scene in the film is seldom reproduced, however. It deserves a closer look, as it set up important themes.

The flat, bleak Kansas terrain is really the first character we meet. A road bisects it. It is bordered by fencing. On the flat picture plane the road is a classic triangular shape receding toward a vanishing point on the horizon line. Da Vinci's "Last Supper" uses this form to suggest infinity. In fact, Nissan borrowed the same concept to create a logo for its Infinity line of luxury vehicles.

33

Dorothy travels on the infinite road, as does everyone who comes into being. The finite earthly journey is part of the larger infinite one. At the moment, Dorothy appears to be moving forward, but is looking backward at the camera, in the direction of the unpleasant encounter she and Toto have just had with Miss Gulch. The musical score lightens the scene; MGM's orchestra plays the beginning of "The Happy Farmer."

Dorothy kneels to examine Toto and delivers her first line, *"She isn't coming yet, Toto. Did she hurt you? She tried to, didn't she?"* Happy and sad, good and evil are often neighbors along life's road. While she moves away from Miss Gulch's pursuit, she runs breathlessly toward those who love and care for her, Uncle Henry and Aunt Em.

Unfortunately, they're busy. It's not that they don't care. Uncle Henry explains, *"Don't bother us now, honey. This incubator's gone bad, and we're likely to lose a lot of our chicks."* No doubt Dorothy is fed from those chickens. Aunt Em and Uncle Henry are busy providing for her, while not providing for her. *"Oh the poor little things,"* Dorothy empathizes. But right now she's got her own troubles. Her story of Miss Gulch hitting Toto with a rake falls on deaf ears. She's interrupting Aunt Em's chick count. *"Seventy!"* Em says, struggling to concentrate. Then, *"Dorothy, please!"* This time, Dorothy gets the message: Get lost!

Most of us have lived in this scene, haven't we, maybe on both ends of this dialogue in the same day? Someone we love hasn't the time for us. When we are young and dependent upon the care of adults this can be very wounding. Poverty can be a big contributor to the problem. Depression-era Kansas was a very forbidding place where keeping food on the table took all the energy parents could muster. Sometimes children grow up to be adults who only remember the words, *Go away!* When that happens, it creates a need for future healing. Dorothy, in the end, will hear Em's voice full of love, pleading, *"Wake up, honey ... Dorothy, dear ... it's Aunt Em, darling."*

Wouldn't it be great if in this life or at some moment along life's infinite way, everyone hears the loving voice of parents, children, spouses or ex-spouses, who were once preoccupied, overwhelmed or for some reason unable to relate to us as we would have wished? Wouldn't it be great if life, in this world or the next, afforded the opportunity for us to start over with each other? I believe it does. Remember the film's dedication to the Young in Heart. That's you. Or it can be, if you want it to be.

If "Not now, I'm busy!" gets repeated too often, then our stories never get heard. For our lives to have meaning we have to experience things, relate our experiences to those around us, and reflect upon what our next action might be. And, of course, we take our turn as listeners and share the experiences and the stories of others. When everybody's busy this process gets cheated and everyone is diminished. Watch for this theme to recur in the film. What happens when people's stories get heard? And what happens when they don't?

Dorothy moves on to the farmhands: Zeke, Hunk and Hickory. The notes in the screenplay tell us something important: They're busy! Dorothy tries to launch into her story. She even solicits advice: *"Zeke, what am I going to do about Miss Gulch? Just cause Toto chases her old cat...."* Again the screenplay notes, he hurries away in midsentence. To make matters worse, Hunk insults her: *"Think you didn't have any brains at all!"* He offers know-it-all advice about avoiding Miss Gulch, delivered with a patronizing attitude. Dorothy replies, *"Oh, Hunk, you just won't listen, that's all."* They're both right. But nobody's listening. Or being heard.

Dorothy idly walks on the pigsty fence, balancing herself, while Zeke blusters about having courage. But Dorothy falls into the pigpen, squealing. Soon Aunt Em is in the middle of it all threatening to fire "three shiftless farmhands," while offering them a snack! *"Can't work on an empty stomach. Have some crullers, just fried,"* she says. You gotta love that Aunt Em. She's saving at-risk chicks, while supervising employees, and frying doughnuts. Incredibly, Dorothy tries again to tell Em her Miss Gulch story, only to be interrupted. *"Now, Dorothy, dear, stop imagining things … you always get yourself into a fret over nothing."*

Ouch! To begin with, she hasn't even heard the story she's discounting. And there really is trouble brewing. But Aunt Em finds the time to point out a character flaw on the fly … Dorothy's a worrywart! *"Now you just help us out today and find yourself a place where you won't get into any trouble!"*

Dorothy asks Toto an existential question: *"Someplace where there isn't any trouble … do you suppose there is such a place, Toto?"*

What do you think? Is there such a place?

CHAPTER 6

Going No Place

Christian spirituality speaks to the issue

of trouble. God chooses to condescend in the best sense of the word: to come down to be with. God will have compassion; that is, he will suffer with the troubled one when there is suffering to undergo. God will be companion; that is, he is one with whom one shares bread. As Aunt Em departs, Dorothy stands looking sadly after her. Dorothy munches her cruller and breaks bread ... with Toto. He eats the morsel as she asks him, *"Someplace where there isn't any trouble ... do you suppose there is such a place, Toto?"* She doesn't listen for his reply.

Earth is immediately eliminated as a possibility in Dorothy's way of thinking. She focuses on something unearthly. Utopian. Ethereal. She's an earthling who's giving up on earth. This troubleless place, she says, *"Can't be gotten to by a boat or train."* And it must be, *"far, far away. Behind the moon, beyond the rain."* Then she breaks into song, pining to go... "Somewhere Over the Rainbow." It's a lovely fantasy, and a still lovelier song, but it's a rather poor strategy for life on Earth.

At Christmas, Christians celebrate an extraordinary event. God chooses to be an earthling. From now on nothing earthly will be foreign to God, and God won't be an extraterrestrial (literally, one from off of *terra*, the earth). From now on God can be our constant companion, as Toto is to Dorothy. Our journey is still ours to choose, and we can even choose some kind of unreality if we want. But it would be best if we'd stay grounded, while reaching for the stars. A star, our sun, lights our way every morning and the dreams that we dare to dream really do come true. Many earthlings who've never been behind the moon can attest to that.

Still, life can be painful and lonely and escaping from it in one manner or another can be very appealing. Especially when storm clouds gather. And they're gathering for Dorothy.

Let's go back to the scene where all this trouble started. Look carefully as Miss Gulch stiffly rides her bicycle toward the Gale home on her nasty errand. She carries a rolled-up umbrella strapped to the handlebar. One gets the impression that she brings a dark cloud with her wherever she goes.

"Mr. Gale," she calls out, greeting Uncle Henry. This suggests either that he is Dorothy Gale's blood uncle, or that he has adopted her. We are not told. By the time that Miss Gulch's visit is complete, the dirty deed is done. Toto is put in her basket to be taken away and destroyed. Off she goes, leaving Dorothy in tears. Henry and Em offer only feeble resistance, for they, *"can't go against the law."*

Miss Gulch is seen riding away with Toto, the basket containing him strapped to the back of the bicycle. But the lid is bumping up and down; the catch comes loose and Toto escapes. He streaks back to Dorothy, who is crying on her bed. The screenplay notes read, "Toto barks, as he hurtles through the open window in one wild leap and lands on the bed." Dorothy realizes almost immediately that, *"They'll be coming back for you in a minute."* Who are "they"? Certainly Miss Gulch. Uncle Henry and Aunt Em? The sheriff? Have you ever felt "they" are all against you, that there is no one left on your side? Dorothy feels utterly unsupported. She makes a critical decision: *"We've got to run away!"*

40

How much of the world's suffering has its origins in the conclusion that "I've got to run away!" Surely flight has its merits. I was once in an intolerable situation, which was making my life miserable. One of my religious brothers knew a little about my struggle and inquired about it. I told him I had the opportunity to leave the situation, but that I felt that to do so would be running away. In my mind at that time, I thought that running away involved cowardice or the shirking of duty, and I said so. He replied, "running away isn't always a bad thing. It's wise to run out of a burning building." Good point! I said, "well, I'm not burned to a crisp yet, but I'm certainly toasted." I ended up exercising an option to move on, which led to a wonderful new path for the next decade of my life. I was fortunate not merely to have had something to leave behind, but something to move toward. Dorothy has nowhere to go. She runs *away*, but not *toward*. Now she's on a road to anywhere or nowhere.

And in the next scene she's on a road that appears to go nowhere. The screenplay suggests that, "Dorothy and Toto look very small against the immensity of the prairie, which spreads out in every direction."

This predicament is a critical universal theme, which I think accounts for the enormous popularity and effectiveness of this story. The world is full of individual running-away stories. Some we've survived to look back upon. But many are ongoing, fraught with danger and suffering, with no happy ending in sight. When we have no one to turn to, running away may be running toward something pain-numbing. Alcohol and drug abuse is a well-trod road. In fact, Judy Garland as Dorothy gave the film poignancy, during her lifetime, as her struggles with booze and pills were well-chronicled in the tabloid press. Running away might involve seeking solace with a "any port in a storm" mentality. Many people end up in abusive relationships, which began with a desperate need to belong somewhere. Some run away into their work, because their home life is so dissatisfying. Others see no road ahead at all and try to end their lives to make the pain stop.

As a pastoral minister, I am reminded that *pastor* means, "shepherd." A pastoral heart wants to guide people to safety, and maybe to even more than that. In one of the Bible's most beloved passages, Psalm 23, God speaks as a shepherd, who will stand between us and any enemies. A shepherd soul stares down the wolves for the sake of the beloved. A shepherded soul need not necessarily know where the road ahead leads for, "You guide me along the right path. Even though I walk through a dark valley [or an enchanted forest with lions and tigers and bears, oh my!] I fear no evil for you are at my side … to give me courage."

I'm hoping as I write this book that people who are running away will ask for blessed companionship. It could come through conventionally religious channels, for the Spirit of God can be found in faith-based bodies. God, however, can be found in the oddest places in the oddest forms. I believe that Dorothy can say, "I fear no evil, for you are at my side." Who is at her side to give her courage? Toto, for starters. There will be others along the way, all of them blessed and flawed or flawed and blessed. The first person she and Toto encounter will be well-acquainted with aimless wandering. In fact, he will be an old homeless guy camping out in a ditch. Meet Professor Marvel.

CHAPTER 7

Marvelous Encounter

Recall that *The Wizard of Oz*

was published in 1900 at the conclusion of one era and the beginning of another. Professor Marvel is old. Dorothy is young. The 19th-century American archetype for flight was "running away to join the circus." A lifetime of running away has landed this man in a dusty gully, with only his horse for company. The coat he wears suggests faded glory. In fact MGM's wardrobe people searched Hollywood thrift stores looking for the Professor's coat. Only later was it discovered that, sewn into the lining, was the name "L. Frank Baum." The author's own coat — perhaps given to charity after his death 20 years earlier — made it into the film by coincidence.

We learn from the faded lettering on his carnival wagon that he has been "acclaimed by the crowned heads of Europe." That's another running-away strategy — when you think you're living the life of a nobody, associate yourself with a Somebody and lose yourself in them. Professor Marvel can read your past and future in his crystal ball. He can juggle for you too, if you like. On the side of the wagon he's identified as a balloon exhibitionist, a talent that will come in handy later.

But for now, he, Dorothy and Toto must get acquainted. He sizes up Dorothy as a kindred spirit doing what he did decades ago, running away. *"Now, why are you running away? No, no, now don't tell me. They ... they don't understand you at home...."*

That's an interesting word, *understand*. It implies that an understood person stands upon a foundation provided by those beneath them. Sometimes we hear references from grateful people, perhaps when being honored for a great accomplishment, that they stand on the shoulders of those who came before them. Think of those persons who have held you up, who have stood under you, supported you. For the moment, no one stands under Dorothy. She thinks she's on her own, without support. *"They don't appreciate you* (which means to *help increase in value*)," the Professor continues. *"Why, it's just like you could read what was inside of me,"* Dorothy responds in what the screenplay calls, "awed tones."

The Professor needs no crystal ball to read what's inside her. He knows a fellow traveler when he sees one — and he has compassion. Toward the end of his own life's journey he knows better than to chase after the rainbow's end. He tries to help her appreciate the love and support she does have even if it seems painfully insufficient.

Toto identifies the Professor as a companion — one with whom we break bread — by grabbing a wienie right off his fork. *"He's perfectly welcome! As one dog to another,"* the Professor laughs. Dorothy sees him as a potential companion, too, and suggests, *"Oh please, Professor, why can't we go with you and see all the crowned heads of Europe?" "Do you know any?"* he replies, forgetting himself momentarily. *"Oh, you mean the thing,"* pointing to the faded lettering on the side of his wagon. *"I never do anything without consulting my crystal first. Let's go inside…."*

The screenplay notes describe the wagon's interior as, "fitted up with the usual hocus-pocus, such as a fortune-telling booth." *Hocus-pocus* is defined as "nonsense or sham, used especially to cloak deception." It's a corruption of *hoc est corpus meum*, Latin for *this is my body*, the words of Jesus repeated by the priest at the heart of the Christian Eucharist. I believe them to describe something real, true and intimate. Nevertheless, some see in religious ritual only sham and deception. Professor Marvel, though benevolent, uses religious imagery as a humbug. He dons a headdress, lights two candles and calls to mind, *"the priests of Isis and Osiris in the days of the pharaohs of Egypt, and so on and so on."* He suggests to Dorothy that she'd better close her eyes for a moment, *"in order to be better in tune with the infinite."* The screenplay notes, that, "he rummages through her basket and flips out a photograph." It is a picture of Dorothy and Aunt Em, obviously a treasure among the very few possessions collected as she fled.

Though Professor Marvel sees nothing in that crystal ball, he sees Dorothy's heart clearly enough. He invites her to reach out into the infinite — *within.* Now he's behaving like a true priest even if he is surrounded by hocus-pocus. He helps her focus on the picture of the person who loves her most dearly. *"There is a woman,"* he says. *"She's wearing a polka-dot dress. Her face is careworn."* (Isn't that a lovely synonym for wrinkled? Em earned those wrinkles by caring.) *"That's Aunt Em!"* Dorothy cries. *"What's she doing?"* *"Why, she's crying,"* he answers. *"Someone has hurt her... someone has just about broken her heart."* *"Me?"* Dorothy asks in a small, guilty voice. *"Well, it's someone she loves very much ... someone she's taken care of in sickness."* Sickness is one arena in which love gets tested, isn't it? Marriage vows always include a promise to love the spouse "in sickness and in health." Dorothy is being invited to reflect upon her experiences of being loved, even by flawed people. *"I had the measles once ... and she stayed by me every minute!"*

The Professor continues, *"What's this? Why she's ... she's putting her hand on her heart! Why, she's dropping down on the bed!"* At this point Professor Marvel says,

"That's all. The crystal's gone dark." *"Oh, you don't suppose she could be really sick, do you?"* Dorothy responds. *"Oh, I've got to go home right away! Come on, Toto! Come on!"*

The suggestion that a loved one from whom we're estranged may be seriously ill, even dying, can be a strong motivator. Not every reunion attempt will have a Hollywood ending. We may not be able to do everything, but doing something is a start. In Dorothy's case, her heart is in the right place. It's steering her toward home, but events beyond her control will cause her plans to be delayed. *"A storm's blowin' up, a whopper,"* Professor Marvel says to his horse. *"Poor little kid! I hope she gets home all right."*

I hope that, too, for all of us. I hope that we all get home all right. And I believe we will, in time or outside of it, if our hearts are in the right place. 🐾

CHAPTER 8

A Storm's Blowin' Up

A storm's blowin' up alright,

a whopper. The cyclone is obviously a critical element in the Oz story. It deserves our attention.

Dorothy is caught up in a whirl of emotions. First she feared for Toto's safety, then she became frustrated at having her concerns ignored by those she relied upon. Nobody listened. Flight seemed her best option, and so she ran. Having barely gone a short distance away she is turned around by the suggestion that Aunt Em is suddenly stricken. Now she's running home frantically. Dorothy's world is spinning wildly. Toto is in danger but Aunt Em might be dying. While the skies around her grow dark and ominous, Dorothy is already caught in her own private cyclone.

A cyclone is a volume of air circling around an area of low atmospheric pressure. The word may have several derivations, all from the Greek. *Kyklon* is circular motion; *cyclos* is the coils of a snake. *Cyclops* is the one-eyed mythical beast. The tropical cyclone or hurricane is known for its center of circulation called the eye. The cyclone has tremendous energy that is both focused and potentially destructive. It is both highly organized and chaotic.

We use the language of "highs" and "lows" to describe our emotional states and our successes and failures. We can be "flying high" when all is well, or hitting "rock bottom" like an addict, or being in "the depths of depression." At the heart of a cyclone a center of low pressure sucks the surrounding air into itself. Another thing about cyclones: They're huge cones. They're open at the top where they

51

feed on the energy of dark clouds. At the bottom they touch the earth at a single point. And where they do they leave a big mess.

I think I've experienced this pattern in my own life. Have you? Begin with an area of low pressure, sometimes called a disturbance. Fear. Isolation. Dread. Maybe it starts with some slight or injustice, real or imagined. Add brooding resentment, the beginnings of a grudge. Envy works too, as does betrayal. Low self-esteem can be the center of circulation. Before long there's circular thinking and a painful sense of being trapped by forces beyond our control. Relationships cool and depression clouds clear understanding. Too often alcohol or mood-altering drugs seem a short-term relief, only to add misery, if not rage and violence. The sense of being grounded, of belonging to a place, a person, a people, to oneself, to God or the universe is reduced to a single point, the eye of the storm. And even that may leave the ground and sweep us away.

Let's return to Dorothy now. Cyclones don't just spin in circles. They also travel along a path. She had that odd encounter with Professor Marvel and his crystal ball. It ended with the image of beloved Aunt Em clutching her heart and falling onto the bed. That stirs Dorothy's compassion and prompts a quick about-face. Now she hurries home as fast as she can. Love gives her the power to reverse her direction.

In the story, Dorothy's troubles are placed in the context of everyone else's. The chickens scurry, the horses run loose and the farmhands chase after them.

Aunt Em is panicky. *"I can't find Dorothy!"* she cries. *"She's somewhere out in the storm."*

"Gosh, we can't look for her now!" Henry says, taking charge. *"Come on! Get in the cellar! Hurry up!"*

Dorothy arrives home at this point, the cyclone's winds swirling around her. In one fleeting scene she puts down her suitcase and scoops up Toto. She literally lets go of her "baggage" and embraces what she values most. Television news reports often show tornado survivors huddled in the rubble of their houses, having "lost everything," while embracing the families and friends they love.

As Dorothy opens the screen door, it flies off in the wind. Calling out for Auntie Em and Uncle Henry, she's too late. They're in the storm cellar and the cyclone's noise is deafening. She rushes back into the house, to her bedroom. Toto is with her. A blast of wind hits the house; the window blows in and hits Dorothy in the back of the head. She, not Aunt Em, ends up being the one collapsing onto the bed.

As awful as all of this is, *The Wizard of Oz* remains a children's story, and a hopeful one at that. In the next scene we travel with Dorothy and Toto inside the cyclone.

The eye of the storm is that place of stillness at the center of the tempest. Every spiritual path I know of describes a place of stillness accessible through prayer or meditation. As a Christian, I believe that God is always with me in the raging storm and in the still point at its center. "If I fly to the heavens you are there. If I go down to the nether world you are there." (Psalm 139:7-10)

Remember, "Dorothy" means "gift of God." You and I, our lives, are God's gift. Say that to yourself three times, through gritted teeth if you have to: "I am God's gift to the world. I am God's gift to the world. I am God's gift to the world." Remember, "Toto" means "everything." There is only One who is everything. And that One is with all of us. Always and everywhere.

Dorothy and Toto are in the middle of a world of trouble. Looking out her bedroom window she peers down at the swirling funnel. *"We must be up inside the cyclone,"* she shouts. But this is not just her private worst-case scenario. A henhouse floats by. A rooster crows. An old lady knitting in her rocking chair waves a greeting. Two guys in a rowboat tip their hats. We're never alone. Not even in the eye of the storm.

The threat of real evil has a place in the scene, too, for not all that frightens us is imaginary. Some things that are scary are very real indeed. Miss Gulch rides by on her bicycle. She was last seen trying to carry Toto to his death. Dorothy was not "imagining things" as a harried Aunt Em said. Not every low-pressure system spawns cyclones; they must be fed the proper fuel to become tempests. Miss Gulch was a real threat. But the cyclone's building fury magnifies her malevolence. In Dorothy's mind she morphs into The Wicked Witch of the West.

In Dorothy's case, Professor Marvel got it right without consulting his crystal ball. He just looked at the circling clouds and said, *"A storm's blowin' up alright, a whopper."*

CHAPTER 9

Over the
Rainbow

All that glitters is not gold.

The grass is always greener on the other side...

Be careful what you ask for.

"Birds fly over the rainbow. Why, oh why, can't I?"

It was the dream of a place where there isn't any trouble that captured Dorothy's imagination. Haven't the rest of us shared that dream at one time or another? The first criteria for creating utopia is locating it somewhere other than here and now. That's particularly appealing when our here and now is stormy, full of pain and confusion.

Dorothy lands in Oz, a place that's perfectly beautiful at first. Soon, though, it's fraught with trouble. And before you know it, she's saying, *"Oh, I'd give anything to get out of Oz altogether; but which is the way to Kansas? I can't go the way I came!"* She'll be directed to follow a glittery golden pathway to a city greener than emeralds and a wizard with all the answers to life's questions. Is life simply chasing one rainbow after the next?

"The house spins up in the swirling funnel of the cyclone," the screenplay notes read, "and then parts company with it. The house begins to fall, spirals down through the air and comes to a crashing halt."

A crashing halt.

Here I want to pause and remind you of my purpose in writing about *The Wizard of Oz*. It's been seen by more people than any movie ever made. It's been taken to heart by millions.

Why?

I'm no wizard, but I think some pieces of that puzzle can be found in Munchkinland. Three very human emotions converge in Munchkinland: disappointment, disillusionment and disorientation.

• **Disappointment derives from the idea of being removed from an appointed office or a status to which we feel entitled.** The mind escapes the present moment and runs ahead to some future place or state, endowing it with every imaginable good. Today's troubles are replaced with tomorrow's allurements. But as tomorrow becomes today the dream loses its luster, and we're disappointed.

• **Disillusionment goes beyond mere disappointment.** An illusionist performs trickery and sleight of hand, deliberately creating a false impression. The illusionist mocks, and often profits, at the expense of the fool who falls for a bill of goods. This was Professor Marvel's trade, remember?

• **Disorientation is Dorothy's immediate problem.** She has been spun around; she's dizzy. She's no longer sure where she is. To be oriented means, literally, "to face the east," that part of the sky where the sun, reliably, invites us to begin the new day. But, then, that only applies on Earth. Not over the rainbow.

AND TOTO, TOO

Clutching Toto in her arms, Dorothy takes her first steps in an unearthly world. She crosses the threshold. What had been her home is now a broken shell. All that is bleak is left behind. A strange light beckons. The Technicolor process was new in 1938. Most film audiences had never seen a movie in color. MGM used the new technology to great effect by having Dorothy pass from black and white dustbowl Kansas into the brilliant colors of Munchkinland.

Dorothy is human. That word derives from *humus*, meaning soil, earth, ground. Dorothy is an earthling, now ungrounded. She has been fashioned from the earth; she's made of its elements. But now she is out of place. As she moves into a landscape of huge flowers and quaint Munchkin architecture she announces, with insight into the obvious, *"Toto, I've a feeling we're not in Kansas anymore. We must be over the rainbow!"*

Suddenly a "large, pink-tinted crystal bubble" approaches, born on a breeze. Glinda the Good Witch arrives. Dorothy has been in this dream-come-true place for one minute and 14 seconds (I counted), when the first person she meets asks, *"Are you a good witch or a bad witch?"*

Bad witches? Wasn't this supposed to be the place where there isn't any trouble?

*"Well, I'm a little muddled — the Munchkins called me because a new witch has just dropped a house on the Wicked Witch of the East — and there's the house — and here **you** are — and that's all that's left of the Wicked Witch of the East,"* Glinda explains.

Death — Toto's and maybe Aunt Em's — had Dorothy chasing around in circles back in Kansas. Death is here too, over the rainbow. There's a dead witch, her feet and ruby red slippers poking out from under the house. And Dorothy is lauded as her killer!

"The Munchkins are happy because you freed them from the Wicked Witch of the East," Glinda informs Dorothy. *"You are their national heroine, my dear."*

Dorothy breaks into song, explaining, *"The wind began to switch, the house to pitch."* The Munchkins join in, *"The kitchen took a slitch. It landed on the Wicked Witch in the middle of a ditch. Which was not a healthy sitch-Uation for the Wicked Witch."*

Next someone's handing her flowers, thanking her for, *"doing it so neatly. You've killed her so completely that we thank you very sweetly."* Glinda announces, *"Let the joyous news be spread, the Wicked Old Witch at last is dead!"* The celebration continues.

This reminds me of a Biblical parallel. It's a celebratory hymn in the Book of Revelation, Chapter 12. The devil, "who deceived the whole world, was thrown down to earth." The heavenly hosts rejoice, because, "Now have salvation and power come, and the kingdom of our God and the authority of his Anointed. For the accuser of our brothers is cast out, who accuses them before our God day and night. They conquered him by the blood of the Lamb and by the word of their testimony; love for life did not deter them from death. So rejoice, you heavens, and you who dwell in them."

The hymn concludes, *"But woe to you, earth and sea, for the Devil has come down to you in great fury, for he knows he has but a short time."*

The Munchkins' song relates that The Wicked Witch has, *"gone where the goblins go, below, below, below."* The Coroner, after his thorough examination, attests that, *"she's not only MERELY dead, she's really most SINCERELY dead."*

The celebration reaches a crescendo with a "terrific explosion." The Munchkins tremble in terror. Dorothy clings to Toto. From a cloud of sulphrous smoke emerges The Wicked Witch of the West.

Her first words accuse: *"Who killed my sister? Who killed the Witch of the East?"* Pointing a green finger tipped by a sharp green nail she asks Dorothy, *"Was it you?"*

"No, No! It was an accident — I didn't mean to kill anybody!" Dorothy replies, trembling.

"Well, my little pretty," the witch sneers, *"I can cause accidents, too!"*

Glinda, that airborne, feminine source of comfort and wisdom, asks, *"Aren't you forgetting the ruby slippers?"*

Instantly the slippers appear on Dorothy's feet, grounding her for the journey ahead. They are a gift endowed with gifts. *"Keep tight inside them — their magic must be very powerful, or she wouldn't want them so badly,"* Glinda says.

The ruby slippers have become iconic. When I've taught adult confirmation classes to college students, I've used them as an illustration. Catholic Christians are often baptized in infancy. We believe God endows us with all of the gifts of the Holy Spirit. Some time later in life, the baptized person is confirmed and these gifts are in some way strengthened and made firm. Seven gifts are listed in Scripture: wisdom, knowledge, understanding, counsel, piety, courage and awe. I think of them as latent in the soul. They are activated when the need arises. We can't know ahead of time every resource we'll need in life. Within us are the gifts, which will manifest when needed. In my interpretation of the story, Dorothy walks now, not in magic shoes, but in spiritual gifts, which her future challenges, will call forth.

The Wicked Witch promises to provide some of those challenges. She'll bide her time. *"But just try to stay out of my way — just try! I'll get you, my pretty, and your little dog, too!"* With a burst of mocking laughter and some theatrics — smoke, fire and a thunderclap — she's gone. For now.

Glinda advises Dorothy that she'd best be on her way. *"I'm afraid you've made rather a bad enemy of the Wicked Witch of the West. The sooner you get out of Oz altogether, the safer you'll sleep, my dear."* When Dorothy relates that she can't go back the way she came, she states what I think is one of the story's universals. Life can't be lived in reverse. Even going home means moving forward.

Though I think Glinda is in some ways wise, she's also capable of being *"a little muddled."* Near the film's climax she'll tell Dorothy, *"You don't need to be helped any longer. You've always had the power to go back to Kansas."* Well, why didn't she just say so in the first place? When pressed, she'll say that her earlier advice about consulting The Wizard was because, *"She wouldn't have believed me. She had to learn it for herself."*

Maybe. But for now Dorothy is led to believe that the knowledge and power she needs is outside of herself. There's this Wizard. He's supposedly, *"very good, but very mysterious."* What is known of him is hearsay. As the song says, *"We hear he is Whiz of a Wiz, if ever a Whiz there was."* It seems he lives in this Emerald City, not here. Dorothy asks, *"But how do I start for Emerald City?"* Glinda, in her lilting way, replies, *"It's always best to start at the beginning… Follow the Yellow Brick Road."*

And so the journey begins again. The Munchkins sing, *"You're off to see the Wizard, the Wonderful Wizard of Oz."* In English, the pronoun **you** can be either singular or plural. (Sometimes the plural becomes "you all," "y'all" or "youse guys.") I think the Munchkins mean singular; Dorothy is setting off. But she's already accompanied. Toto is with her always. Others will be, too, as the journey unfolds. For now, there's nothing left to do but follow. Follow. Follow. Follow.

CHAPTER 10

Spiraling

When I was a kid my parents saw that I had

some budding artistic talent. One Christmas they got me a "Spirograph." It was a set of colored ballpoint pens, drawing paper and a series of flat plastic shapes whose edges had little gearlike teeth. These shapes were pinned to the pad. A second little plastic gear was placed against the first one. This one had little holes just large enough to put the pen point through. The idea was to make one disc go around the other, allowing the pen to create these colorful geometric spirals. You never really knew what you were creating until you were through.

As long as you were careful and kept the little gear-teeth engaged, the pattern would unfold with beautiful order. Later, in high school, I learned that these shapes had names like *parabolas*, which, it turns out, have complex mathematical lives. Satellites, cellphones and the Internet all work because somebody figured out all these patterns in the universe and built technologies around them.

Mostly I just doodled. And sometimes I didn't even do that very well. If you weren't careful the little gears would disengage and send the pen careening off in a pattern-spoiling direction. In ink.

Much of life is lived in ink.

But not all of it. If you screw up today, there's always tomorrow. God, the universe and loving, patient people all will tell you the same thing: Turn the paper over and start again.

Dorothy regretted her decision to run away almost as soon as she'd made it. Then, she turned around. There's a religious word for that: *repent*. It doesn't presume shame or groveling. It just means turning around.

Turning around can give you a new and possibly life-changing point of view. Mind if I tell you a story of a time when I turned around?

It was a hot summer, even for Arizona. Day after day we had highs above 110. It was hard to breathe and hard to move. The news that summer was breathtakingly awful. Each morning I awoke to headlines about priests sexually abusing children. In our local diocese the bishop and the district attorney were involved in a bitter exchange played out in the media. It went on and on.

And on Sundays my people would arrive for Mass and slump into their seats looking shell-shocked and exhausted. They looked to me for something; I wasn't sure what. I was as exhausted as they were. What did I have to give them?

Then our bishop was involved in a fatal hit-and-run traffic accident. He was arrested. I watched it on CNN.

Finally, a young man high on drugs found his way into our recently restored historic church. He spent hours breaking stained glass windows and reducing the altar to splinters. (Days later, in his right mind, he turned around. He came back and apologized to me.)

It was now late summer; time to welcome the incoming freshmen and to begin the school year. My tank was empty. I was running on fumes.

I wasn't sleeping well and was waking up tired. Before bedtime one night I told the Lord that I'd had it. "You know how much energy I need to start the school year. I don't have any energy at all. You'd better give me some fast. Goodnight."

Somewhere in the wee hours of the morning I found myself standing in Anacoco Creek. When I was a kid we'd go there after an exhausting summer day of baling hay. The water was up to my chest, but it wasn't refreshing. I was facing downstream. The water was flowing through me and I was bleeding energy. Life was seeping out of me and disappearing downstream. Standing in midstream I was being drained.

Then I heard a voice, and an invitation.

"Nathan, turn around."

I turned around.

I saw a sparkling river of love and life and energy flowing toward me. I couldn't see its source. It was pouring in, over and around me and I was free to soak up all that I could contain. I was a sponge, oversaturated. I couldn't hold another drop.

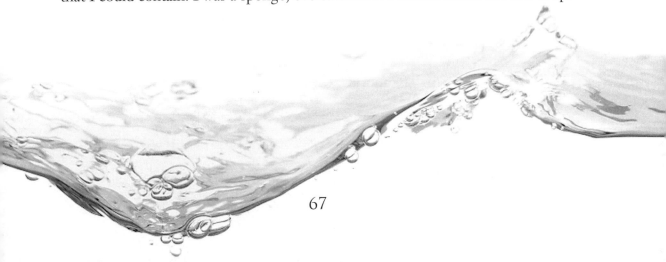

I woke up. I was wide awake, refreshed. And I was ready to start the school year. All I'd needed to do was turn around.

The whole universe is turning around. In fact, "universe" means one turning. Our ancient ancestors observed the heavenly bodies turning in beautiful, reliable order. Nothing could be more natural. Even if I insist on being immovable I can't stop the world from turning. Were I to spend my whole life in one spot, I'd never, ever occupy the same place in time or space, because the Earth is spinning on its axis, creating day and night. And it's circling the sun, creating year after year. And our solar system is part of a galaxy gracefully spiraling around something far too distant for our strongest telescopes to pinpoint.

We're all cosmic travelers whether we like it or not. In the middle of Munchkinland we're standing at the center of a colorful spiral. The Yellow Brick Road begins here. The spiral pattern reappears in the lollipops Dorothy receives as a gift. It's in the DNA helix that's in all your genes. It's in the very universe we're dwelling in and in the microscopic world that pulses through our bloodstream. Even when we think life is "spiraling out of control," it's really not. Think of that song from the '60s that quotes the Book of Ecclesiastes, "To everything, turn, turn, turn, there is a season, turn, turn, turn, and a time for every purpose under heaven."

We might slip a gear from time to time and make a stray mark on the page. When we do, all we have to do is turn around and around and around like Dorothy taking her first circling steps. Soon the path straightens and we're on our way, a part of something beautiful we're in the process of creating.

CHAPTER 11

Life's Way

Dorothy skips through the gate at the edge

of Munchkinland, dancing toward the viewer, then the camera pans to show the vastness of Oz and the Yellow Brick Road diminishing to a point on the distant horizon. This reminds me of the film's opening scene. When we first met Dorothy she was on that road that suggested infinity. She was on her way home.

Then there was the "running away" road, which I've always assumed must have been in the opposite direction of Miss Gulch. But then Dorothy turns around and tries to go home, only to have the cyclone take her somewhere else. She's in that somewhere else only briefly before she's shown the next road and encouraged to follow, follow, follow it. And off she goes.

The Wizard of Oz is an odyssey story. It's a travel narrative full of adventure. The people in an odyssey story are shaped by the travails and triumphs of the journey. In such stories the cast of characters broadens with each new turn in the road.

The screenplay of the MGM film retelling of *The Wizard of Oz* uses this structure:

Prologue (Kansas)

The Main Body of the Story, a linearly driven plot featuring a road moving toward a city of destiny (Oz)

Epilogue (Kansas)

The decision to move from black and white to color and back to black and white emphasizes this structure in the film.

I'll draw some parallels between *The Wizard of Oz* and the story of Jesus as told in the four gospels.

Of the four gospels in the Christian Bible, three — Mark, Matthew and Luke — are organized around a linear understanding of space and time common to the rationalism prevalent in Western thought. Eastern philosophies and spiritualities often emphasize the circular nature of the cosmos and of time. The fourth gospel, John, is more at home in that world. I've developed themes of circularity in describing the cyclone and the spiral. Now I want to turn to the linear.

We're born, we live and we die along a time line. The most concise summation of a human life can be found on a tombstone. Three of the four essential elements of my marker's inscription are already known. At the top will go my name. Just below and to the left will go the year of my birth, 1956, followed by a small line, a hyphen representing my mortal life's duration. To the right of that will go the year of my death, as yet undetermined (TBA).

Matthew's gospel is most like that. It begins with a prestory, chapters 1 and 2, describing the birth of Jesus. Joseph is told in a dream that Mary, his wife, "'will bear a son and you are to name him Jesus,'" which means "God saves," "for he will save his people from their sins." Matthew continues, "All this took place to fulfill what the Lord had said through the prophet: 'Behold the virgin shall be with child and bear a son, and they shall name him Emmanuel,' which means 'God is with us.'"

AND TOTO, TOO

By Chapter 3, Jesus is an adult on a road, gathering traveling companions and moving toward a city of destiny. He dies there, in Jerusalem, in the penultimate chapter, Chapter 27. The reason this story is called *gospel*, which means "good news" is that this death, though real, is only temporary. Jesus stands with his companions at the end of the epilogue, Chapter 28, now risen from the dead. He instructs them to tell this good news to everyone in the world. Death, like birth, is temporary. Both are followed by new life.

Earlier in this story, Jesus' companions have shown themselves to be heartless, brainless and especially cowardly. They all ran away. But they're lovable and loved and he wants to be at home in them always, now and until the end of time. I believe we're all meant to be central characters in this cosmic story.

As Dorothy sets out on her new journey, she'll begin gathering traveling companions with each new turn in the road. The film will devote scenes of approximately equal length to the introductions of The Scarecrow, The Tin Man and The Cowardly Lion. But there's a companion already with us whom we've known since the opening scene. Could we get to know him better?

When I pray, I often say to God, "I love you, but I want to love you more." God is so vast … could we ever love God completely? But then, the person you love the most is vast, too. Lovers can spend a lifetime, maybe even an eternal lifetime, loving their beloved more and more. Can you ever finish loving those you love? Why would you want to?

Dorothy's companion all along has been Toto. She loves him enough to risk her life to save him. Ironically, at a very dark moment, he'll risk his life to save her. There's more to this character, who has been a part of our story since the beginning. It's time to take a closer look at Toto. ❧

CHAPTER 12

Do You Believe in Dog?

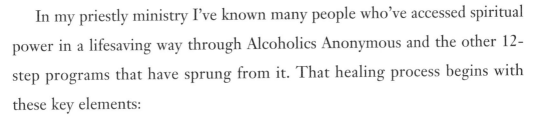

This joke has made the rounds.

Have you heard it?

Q: How can you recognize an agnostic, dyslexic, insomniac?

A: He lies awake every night wondering if there is a Dog.

In my priestly ministry I've known many people who've accessed spiritual power in a lifesaving way through Alcoholics Anonymous and the other 12-step programs that have sprung from it. That healing process begins with these key elements:

One's identity or personhood.

The naming of a critical flaw.

The acknowledgement of the truth of one's powerlessness.

And the seeking of the help of one's higher power (God as one understands God).

The steps are taken with the support of similarly flawed companions and the help of one's higher power. No one tells you that your idea of your higher power must conform to another's orthodoxy. You're not kicked out of the meeting if your idea of your higher power strikes someone else as blasphemous. There's too much at stake for theological squabbling. Addictions kill people and create lots of collateral damage. The healing track record of the 12-step movements is all the proof I need that God says to broken humanity, "Call me whatever you want, but *call* me!"

My higher power is Jesus, who I believe is God made human. I celebrate Christmas because I believe God, who is often thought to be distant and powerful (like The Wizard of Oz), is also with us and is willing to be weak. God is love. Love unites persons, and to love, you must let yourself be vulnerable and weak. God is no exception. It makes no sense to say, "I will love you but I must be in control of our relationship at every moment." Lovers lead *and* follow. Love conquers *and* surrenders. When couples pledge their love and promise to be with their beloved in good times and bad, in sickness and health, until death do us part, I believe they're surrendering themselves into a harmony built into the universe by its creator.

Jesus, famous for all kinds of miraculous power, lays it all down and loves his companions by standing up to oppressive powers. "Kill me if you want," Jesus says, "but I'll be faithful to those I love." That includes his heavenly Father, his disciples, his betrayer and the guy who drives the nails into his hands and feet. And I believe *that* love extends to everybody in the universe. It's not my business to limit God's love or to say that these conditions must first be met for you to qualify as a candidate for God's love. I'm not in charge of your idea of your higher power. I'm a Catholic. That word means universal. I believe God loves everybody wildly, extravagantly, beyond belief and beyond belief systems.

Jesus is sometimes called the human face of God. In this chapter I'll describe the canine face of God: Toto.

In *The Wizard of Oz* I believe he is the higher power, God with us, love enfleshed.

Toto is omnipresent. He's with Dorothy always, on the earth or off of it, in good times and in bad. He's in every scene. He leaves Dorothy only once, and then to save her. She's trapped in the witch's castle, separated from her friends. The witch puts Toto in a basket and commands Nikko, the leader of the flying monkeys, to, *"Throw that basket in the river and drown him!"*

"No! No — no! Here, you can have your old slippers, but give me back Toto!" Dorothy cries.

But the ruby slippers won't come off Dorothy's feet. Sparks fly when the witch tries to take them. *"Fool ... I should have remembered,"* she says savagely. *"Those slippers will never come off ... as long as you're alive! But that's not what's worrying me ... it's how to do it .... These things must be done delicately, or you hurt the spell."*

Toto escapes the basket and scrambles out the door. *"Run, Toto, run! He got away! He got away!"* Dorothy cries joyfully. The witch seizes the hourglass and flips it over. Blood-red sand begins falling. *"You see that? That's how much longer you have to be alive. And it isn't long, my pretty, it isn't long!"*

Meanwhile, as the Winkie guards hurl spears at him, Toto is leaping the moat. He finds Dorothy's companions and calls them to their mission. Then he leads them to Dorothy. He doesn't even have the impressive profile of a grander breed, like the collie-hero, "Lassie" ("What's that, girl? Timmy's fallen down the well?"). But the barking of little Toto, whom The Lion first called "Peewee," is enough to summon the flawed companions, the saving community.

Toto will go with them back into the hellish witch's castle. Later he will be the one to unmask the fraudulent Wizard, that man behind the curtain. He'll leap from the balloon basket, causing Dorothy to follow, and avoid one last ill-fated attempt to get back to Kansas. But I'm getting way ahead of the story. We're just leaving Munchkinland, just starting to follow the Yellow Brick Road. We don't start out on this next part of life's journey alone, though. Even before we meet new companions we've got a fellow traveler, the faithful friend who has been and is always with us: Toto.

I'm not an agnostic; I'm a believer.

I believe in Dog.

CHAPTER 13

At a Crossroads

Dorothy and Toto pass through the gates

of Munchkinland ending one scene and beginning another. Their instructions for the journey consist of one sentence: "Follow the Yellow Brick Road."

If you're following the movie on a DVD, freeze the next frame. Notice in the background the diminishing path they've already trod over hill and dale. In the foreground is an unmarked intersection of roads — yellow brick roads. The screenplay reads, "She stops as the Yellow Brick Road crosses another one. She looks up and down, puzzled."

"Now which way do we go?" Dorothy asks no one in particular.

When I was younger I presumed only one of the roads was the right one, the one that would bring her to her desired destination. That's certainly the way Dorothy sees it as the scene begins.

As a campus minister, I often get to be with young travelers just setting out on their journeys. There are a bewildering number of roads from which to choose. That old question put to children — *What do you want to be when you grow up?* — doesn't belong to the future so much when you have to choose a college or a major. To *be* something in that question means to choose an occupation. To *occupy* means to fill. What you fill your time doing may turn out to be your occupation. But will it be personally fulfilling? And how do you know what to choose?

83

Sometimes students will seek out a priest as someone else might a seer or an oracle. We're supposed to have a hotline to God. Catholic students have sometimes been taught that they have a specific *vocation* (from the word *voice*, calling). God has in mind a perfect life path for them, but they don't know what it is. It's as though life is a search for buried treasure — but without a map.

Back when I was in college I changed majors like I changed clothes. There were so many things to learn about, so many things I might be "when I grew up." I was even beginning to think about *becoming* a priest. Or not, depending upon the day. One day I made an appointment to talk to a priest about it. "How will I know which way to go?" I asked. Do you know what the guy said?

"Follow your joy."

"But I thought I'd have to …."

"Just follow your joy."

At the crossroads it seemed essential that Dorothy choose *the* right path. When she asked aloud, *"Now which way do we go?"* a brainless stranger answered her.

The Scarecrow has grown up to be — a scarecrow. That's both his occupation and his identity. He literally "hangs around" in the corner of this cornfield. His job is to scare the crows away. He's like a nightclub bouncer — made of straw. He's ill-suited to the work. It's "tedious," he explains, and as we come to know him we find he's not at all frightening. He helps Dorothy figure out how to get him down off the pole up his back that has kept him immobile.

A crow lands on him, picks a piece of straw, and flies away, perhaps to build a nest. *"You see, I can't even scare a crow! They come for miles around just to eat in my field and … and laugh in my face.*" He almost weeps. "*Oh, I'm a failure because I haven't got a brain!*"

What he does have, though, is hope, one of the cardinal virtues. For a brainless guy, he's done a lot of thinking up on that pole. He's been introspective. Dorothy asks him a critical question and he has a ready answer.

"*Well, what would you do with a brain if you had one?*"

Immediately we learn that his talent for dancing has been wasted up on that pole. He springs into a bright song and dance, rattling off an impressive rhyming list of things he'd do:

I could while away the hours
Conferrin' with the flowers
Consultin' with the rain
And my head, I'd be scratchin'
While my thoughts were busy hatchin'
If I only had a brain.

By now he has stumbled. Dorothy helps him to his feet, and he continues.

I'd unravel ev'ry riddle
For any individ'le
In trouble or in pain.

85

I like that part. I think he's realizing that he'd make a compassionate counselor. Dorothy sees a future president:

With the thoughts you'd be thinkin'
You could be another Lincoln
If you only had a brain.

Hope is said to "spring eternal." Something beautiful and new springs up within The Scarecrow. It's a sense of endless possibility. Choosing *the* right path just this instant doesn't loom as a terrible, "no-turning-back" moment of decision. Although there is one very important realization he's come to: What he has been doing isn't working. He is at a crossroads.

This young girl and her dog are going to see a wizard. With what the screenplay calls *"a sudden idea"* and what Catholic spiritual theology might call *"a gift of understanding"* The Scarecrow asks, *"Do you think if I went with you this Wizard would give me some brains?"*

"I couldn't say," Dorothy replies. *"But even if he didn't you'd be no worse off than you are now."*

There are a few details to consider. There's this angry witch. But he's not afraid of witches; cowardice is not his problem. He promises he won't try to manage things, *"because I can't think."*

"Won't you take me with you?" The Scarecrow pleads.

"Why of course I will!" Dorothy replies warmly.

"*Hooray!*" The Scarecrow cries, "*We're off to see a Wizard!*" But he sinks down. Dorothy steadies him. "*To Oz!*" she says.

"*To Oz!*" he replies. And they break into the marching song, *We're Off to See the Wizard*.

The funny thing is, as they link arms and set off for the Emerald City they're no longer anxious about wrong turns. They have no map and no GPS. And neither do any of us. Life's possibilities just unfold before us. There's no more discussion of which is the right or wrong way to go. As The Scarecrow had said earlier, "*Of course, people do go both ways!*"

So where did Dorothy's earlier apprehension go? It melted away in the presence of a new companion on the journey. That reminds me of a scene late in the Gospel of John. Jesus is talking to his friends about going on before them, assuring them they are free to follow. But they get scared. One cries out, "But how can we know the way?"

"I am the way," Jesus replies without further directions.

Companionship, having others "along for the ride" of our lives, can take a lot of the fear out of the trip. Most mystical spiritual traditions include some concept of the journey and the destination being one and the same. In any event our travelers, Dorothy, The Scarecrow, and ever-present Toto set out together on the next part of the journey. Full of hope and purpose they have the world at their feet. They're enjoying the moment. And I think they're following their joy. 🐾

CHAPTER 14

Echoes of Eden

Dorothy, The Scarecrow, and Toto

enter a new scene. Look quickly on the left-hand side of the screen to see The Wicked Witch up to no good. She's put a curse on the land. She's in the shadows, behind one of the trees. Then she slinks — or could we say slithers — away.

At the center of this unfolding scene is a young woman reaching for and picking an apple from a tree. Remind you of a Bible story?

In the Eden story we're told that the Lord God created this garden and we are free to eat from any of its trees except one, one which would give us the knowledge of evil (Gen. 2:16-17). The various trees, we're told, "were delightful to look at and good for food" (Gen. 2:9a). Dorothy sees the trees.

"*Oh, apples! Oh … look! Oh! Oh!*" she says with delight. She picks an apple. The tree seizes it in what the screenplay calls, "a claw-like grab," takes it back, and slaps Dorothy's hand.

"*What do you think you're doing?*" the tree demands.

"*We've been walking a long ways, and I was hungry,*" Dorothy replies, shocked to be talking with an angry tree. The tree calls out to its neighbor with biting sarcasm.

"*She was hungry! Well, how would you like to have someone come along and pick something off of you?*"

"*Oh, dear!*" says Dorothy woefully. "*I keep forgetting I'm not in Kansas.*"

The brainless Scarecrow has an idea, a little reverse psychology. "*Come along, Dorothy. You don't want any of those apples. Hmmm!*"

"Are you hinting my apples aren't what they ought to be?" the tree huffs.

"Oh no," The Scarecrow replies, *"It's just that she doesn't like little green worms!"*

The tree grabs Dorothy. She screams. The Scarecrow fights the tree as Dorothy struggles free.

"I'll show you how to get apples," The Scarecrow says to Dorothy. He puts his thumbs in his ears and waggles his fingers like a taunting child.

The tree begins pelting them with the same fruit that, moments before, it wouldn't part with. It didn't want to feed Dorothy but it is very willing to hurl its fruit at her like missiles.

The Scarecrow's plan worked, though, and Dorothy will have her apples. One of them lands at the feet of another new creature who will soon be a friend and traveling companion, The Tin Man.

He creaks almost inaudibly.

"Did you say something?" Dorothy asks.

"Oil can," he creaks, still hoarse.

"Oil can what?" The Scarecrow asks.

Dorothy spies the oil can on a nearby stump. *"Here it is! Where do you want to be oiled first?"* she asks.

Oil is a healing medium. Think of the Holy Oils of a priest. Or of massage oil in the trained

hands of a massage therapist. Dorothy and The Scarecrow oil his mouth, and The Tin Man's story begins to flow as they work his arms and joints. Dorothy lowers the heavy ax.

"Did that hurt?" she asks.

"No, it feels wonderful! I've held that ax up for ages."

"Goodness!" Dorothy replies, *"How did you ever get like this?"*

His answer is simple. He got rained on. *"And right in the middle of a chop, I - I rusted solid. I've been like that ever since."* We don't always need to know a lot of details to be healers.

"Well, you're perfect now." Dorothy proclaims. I hear a creation-story echo. God looked at all he made and called it very good.

"Perfect?" The Tin Man objects. *"Bang on my chest if you think I'm perfect."*

The screenplays reads, "Dorothy raps on his chest, which echoes."

"Beautiful!" The Scarecrow exclaims. *"What an echo!"*

I love that. Others sometimes see goodness in us that we overlook or even deny.

As a high school freshman I hated my body. It was all scrawny and gangly and awkward. Gym class was fifth period. I hated it. I went from there to the last class of the day, algebra. I loved it. Isn't that the definition of a nerd: hates gym, loves algebra? Anyway, algebra was taught by this very kind Irish nun, Sister Brigid. One day I arrived upset enough that she asked what was wrong. I'd failed at something athletic, I don't even remember what, and told her, "It's because I'm so skinny."

"Skinny?" she said. "You're not skinny! You're just wiry!" I can even remember how she set her feminine jaw to make the word sound manly.

That's 40 years ago now and I can remember it like yesterday. That's the power of a healing word.

"Beautiful! What an echo!" The Scarecrow says.

The Tin Man won't hear it.

"It's empty," he says.

Here's what the screenplay says next: "He looks around, then lowers his voice as though telling a terrible secret."

"The Tinsmith forgot to give me a heart."

That's the terrible secret, like the whisper of the serpent to Eve. That damn creator of his screwed up. It's God's fault.

Back in Eden, when things go sour, the blaming begins.

"The serpent tricked me," says Eve to her creator.

"It was that woman you put here," complains Adam.

Can you see yourself in this picture? I can see myself.

The Tin Man may not have a heart, but he knows heartache. With The Scarecrow it was Dorothy asking, *"What would you do with a brain if you had one?"* that prompted his hopeful song and dance. The Tin Man needs no prompting to sing his sad song in a major key.

"When a man's an empty kettle
He should be on his mettle
And yet I'm torn apart
Just because I'm presumin'

That I could be kind-a human
If I only had a heart."

So many people have suffered profoundly during their lives because someone made them feel, or told them explicitly, that they were subhuman. Sometimes Bible verses have been used to underscore the point.

"I'd be tender, I'd be gentle
And awful sentimental
Regarding love and art
I'd be friends with the sparrows
And the boy who shoots the arrows
If I only had a heart."

The Tin Man had rusted into immobility, believing himself to be unlovable. I've known plenty of people like that. You probably have too. Gay people, mixed-race people, depressed people, poor or poorly educated people, overweight people, skinny people, shy people, grieving people, sexually abused people, homeless people and people who seem to have everything going for them.

The Tin Man does a little dance, at times becoming rigid and in danger of falling. But he dances on.

Dorothy and The Scarecrow come to help. He staggers, knocking The Scarecrow over. Finally, the dancing is done.

"Oh, are you alright?" Dorothy asks.

"I'm afraid I'm a little rusty yet," The Tin Man replies. You have to admire his effort.

"That was wonderful!" Dorothy replies. *"We were just wondering why you couldn't come with us to the Emerald City to ask the Wizard of Oz for a heart!"*

The Tin Man responds in the only way a despondent, empty person can, essentially wondering what could go wrong next.

"Well, suppose the Wizard wouldn't give me one once we got there?"

That's why we need each other, don't you think? Because we each take our turn seeing the glass half-empty. Dorothy's argument isn't convincing, but her determination is appealing.

"Oh, but he will!" she says. *"He must! We've come such a long way already."*

But here comes The Wicked Witch again, bursting onto the scene with insults and threats. Sometimes at a critical moment the critic emerges. It may be a person from the "Misery Loves Company" school who doesn't want us to change and leave them behind. Other times it's the devilish voice in our own heads cursing, *"You'll never amount to anything and there's no use trying."*

This Witch tries fire. But it backfires on her. She tries to break up this little band, throwing a fireball at The Scarecrow. But remember, he earlier said he'd face a whole boxful of matches for a chance at having a brain.

Luckily, tin men aren't flammable. Our Tin Man uses his tin hat to extinguish the flames while The Witch vanishes in a puff of smoke.

Sometimes fire reduces hope to ashes. Other times it produces a stronger metal. The Tin Man is tempered into a "man of steel."

"I'm not afraid of her," The Scarecrow says angrily. *"I'll see you reach the Wizard, whether I get a brain or not."*

The Tin Man echoes the thought, *"I'll see you reach the Wizard, whether I get a heart or not."*

"Oh," Dorothy says happily, *"You're the best friends anybody ever had."* Remember, she's saying this to someone who, moments before, thought himself unlovable. *"And it's funny, but I feel as if I've known you all the time — but I couldn't have, could I?"*

Have you ever come to love and be loved so much by someone so that it's hard to imagine your life before they were a part of it?

"I wish I could remember … but I guess it doesn't matter, anyway — we know each other now, don't we?" Dorothy asks.

"That's right," says The Scarecrow.

"We do!" The Tin Man adds, as they all laugh.

"To Oz!" says The Scarecrow, offering Dorothy his arm.

"To Oz!" The Tin Man echoes, offering his arm, too.

The scene is ending. The marching song begins and they're off to see the Wizard. And here, in the middle of our story there's another new beginning. There's another friend to meet, another life about to be changed forever, just a little farther down the road.

CHAPTER 15

Fear
and Courage

Dorothy, Toto, Scarecrow and Tin Man

have just survived a real encounter with the flame-throwing Wicked Witch. Afterward, The Scarecrow, at whom the fireball was directed, declares, *"I'm not afraid of her. I'll see you get safely to the Wizard now."* It's a bold statement about an uncertain future. It sounds courageous, don't you think?

The gospel stories about Jesus and his companions have a similar scene. Jesus knows he has powerful enemies who would like to see him destroyed. They'll probably come after his companions, too.

"'Lord,' Simon Peter said to him, 'where do you mean to go?' Jesus answered him, 'I am going where you cannot follow me now; later on you shall come after me.' 'Lord,' Peter said to him, 'why can I not follow you now? I will lay down my life for you!' 'You will lay down your life for me, will you?' Jesus answered. 'I tell you truly, the cock will not crow before you have three times disowned me.'" (John 13:37-38) And a few hours later Peter will cower in fear, around the glow of a campfire, confronted not by a Wicked Witch, but a little servant girl. (John 18:17-18)

We may successfully stand up to a real threat, only to be scared to death by an imaginary one. That's about to happen to our friends.

Dorothy, Toto, Scarecrow and Tin Man enter a darker part of the forest. The Yellow Brick Road still guides them, although this section of it looks less traveled. "They move forward slowly and stop," the screenplay reads.

"Oh, I don't like this forest! It's — it's dark and creepy!" Dorothy worries, infecting everyone within earshot.

"Of course, I don't know, but I think it'll get darker before it gets lighter," The Scarecrow adds.

"I don't know" is the operative phrase here. If you don't know something, why not keep silent, rather than contribute something negative? Too late now, though. This thing is snowballing.

"Do you suppose we'll meet any wild animals?" Dorothy asks apprehensively.

"Mmm - we might," says The Tin Man who hadn't, until that point, given the matter any thought.

"Animals that — that eat straw?" The Scarecrow adds, his voice trembling.

"Uh, some," says The Tin Man nonchalantly, *"But mostly lions and tigers and bears."*

"Lions?" Dorothy asks with alarm.

"And tigers?" Scarecrow adds tensely.

"And bears," Tin Man nods.

They look around slowly, then start to run deeper into the dark woods, their steps become rhythmic in a crescendo of fear. It's just the opposite of the encouraging marching song, *"We're Off to See the Wizard."* Now they're scaring each other with the chant,

"Lions and tigers and bears. Oh my!

LIONS AND TIGERS AND BEARS. OH MY!

LIONS AND TIGERS AND BEARS. OH MY!"

Do you recognize this pattern in your life? Have you ever talked yourself into being afraid? Or joined your voice to a chorus of doomsayers?

None of this is making much sense. They're not being followed or chased, mind you. So they're not fleeing a real threat to their safety. For all they know they could be running headlong into the very thing they fear. It makes no sense — because it's irrational. A lot of our fears are.

By the end of the scene we'll know that this was all a lot of worrying over nothing. Worry, anxiety and fear always borrow from an uncertain future. Much of the unhappiness I've seen people suffer in the course of my ministry has its roots in this kind of irrational fear. Most of my own worst moments have been riddled with fears.

Wariness is another matter. When the road ahead has probable dangers, wariness causes us to focus our energy in the present moment to face the present challenge. But that's not what our friends are doing here, is it?

The poor Scarecrow first asked if there might be looming animals that eat straw. Strawmen must be wary of straw-eating animals … cows, or goats, maybe. But lions and tigers and bears? They don't even eat straw!

The Tin Woodsman lives in the woods. This is his home turf. Why should he feel unsafe here? He might have reason to fear a sudden cloudburst like the last one that caused him to rust solid. But lions and tigers and bears? They don't eat tin. Besides, he's got an ax, and he knows how to use it. What's he got to be afraid of?

When they do meet up with an initially ferocious lion, look at which of the four end up cowering at The Cowardly Lion's feet: Scarecrow and Tin Man. Fear does that to people.

What happens next could be called, "The Attack of the Dandelion." The Cowardly Lion leaps out of the woods with a well-practiced roar. He straightens up in a boxer's stance and taunts his opponents. Bert Lahr plays this scene perfectly, like a street-smart bully.

"I'll fight ya both together if ya want. I'll fight ya with one paw tied behind my back. I'll fight ya standin' on one foot! I'll fight ya with my eyes closed."

Bullies crave power. They try to suck it out of you, often with insults.

"Get up and fight, ya shiverin' junkyard. Put ya hands up, ya lopsided bag of hay!"

How the mighty have fallen! They stood up well to the real threat of the dangerous Wicked Witch. But they wilt before this windbag. Even he loses interest in them.

The camera then focuses on Toto. He gets a closeup — and a rare speaking part. He barks.

Remember that I think of Toto as a Christ figure, God with us. Toto comes to the defense of his friends. Jesus promised his friends he'd give us an advocate — one who would speak up for us when we're attacked. We call that the Spirit.

The Lion turns to Toto. *"I'll get you anyway, peewee,"* he growls.

Dorothy grabs Toto in her arms and slaps The Lion smartly on the nose. *"Shame on you!"* she says.

The Lion cries, *"What did you do that for? I didn't bite him!"*

"No, but you tried to! It's bad enough picking on a straw man, but when you go picking on poor little dogs—."

Bert Lahr as The Lion bawls hysterically. *"Well, ya didn't have to go and hit me, did ya?"* He sobs, *"Is my nose bleedin'?"* He carries on with such melodrama

104

that he causes young Judy Garland to come out of character ever so slightly. You might have to watch the scene several times to catch it. She holds Toto up to her face to hide a smile, while The Cowardly Lion blubbers.

"Why, you're nothing but a great big coward!" says Dorothy, her fears now forgotten.

Dorothy speaks the truth. The Lion responds to it with relief. *"You're right, I* **am** *a coward! I haven't any courage at all! I even scare myself."*

He may not think he has courage, but he has self-knowledge and honesty.

The Scarecrow in search of a brain has an idea. He says to Dorothy, *"Don't you think the Wizard could help him too?"*

"Well, wouldn't you feel degraded to be seen in the company of a cowardly lion? I would," The Lion sobs.

There's nothing degrading or ugly about truth. Seeing someone acknowledge the truth about something awful has its own beauty. As a priest, I've seen that in confession many times. Don't you think it takes great courage to tell your story publicly, truthfully?

"It's been in me so long, I just gotta tell ya how I feel."

"Well, come on!" Dorothy encourages, taking his arm as they begin walking. The Lion sings his sad story:

"Yeah, it's sad, believe me, missy,
When you're born to be a sissy,
Without the vim and verve.
But I could show my prowess,

Be a lion not a mowess,

If I only had the nerve."

Courage is often thought of as a manly virtue. Men must have made that up. Courage is a human virtue and cowardice, its opposite, is painful to the man, woman or child who is filled with fear. The Lion is not lionhearted; instead he has a wound at the *cor* of his being. *Cor* is Latin for heart, and it's the root of the word *courage*.

When I prepare Catholic college students for the sacrament of confirmation I remind them that courage is one of the seven gifts of the Holy Spirit. God gives this gift to those who ask for it. Growth in courage begins with desire and a decision to seek the thing we desire. Remember, our friends on the Yellow Brick Road are on exactly this quest. They were told about this wizard who dispenses gifts and they're off to ask for his help, now with their new companion, The Lion.

"I'd be brave as a blizzard," he sings.

"I'd be gentle as a lizard," The Tin Man adds.

"I'd be clever as a gizzard," The Scarecrow joins in.

Notice that they don't say, "you'd be gentle" or "you'd be clever." They've made The Lion's struggle their own. They're all seeking *cor-age*. They're all longing to live fully at home in their own heart of hearts. And, of course, so is Dorothy.

But it's Dorothy who contributes the most insightful line. They'll all get what they desire, *"If the Wizard is a wizard who will serve."*

CHAPTER 16

Playing
Witch's Advocate

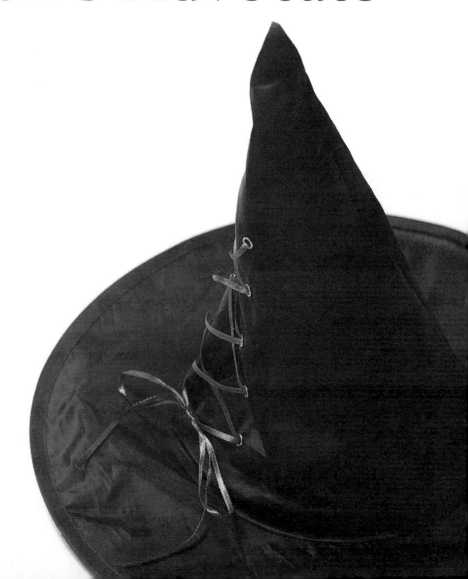

"*Well, we haven't really met properly, have we?*"

Dorothy spoke that line back at the crossroads where she first encountered The Scarecrow. So much has happened since then. They've met and befriended two more companions. Each new character found a compassionate hearing, voiced his heart's desire and was invited to become a part of the shared journey.

By now we've gained insight into all the main characters we've met except one: The Wicked Witch. There have been some ugly encounters with her so far and there will be more to come. But the truth is, no one inside or outside of the story can say they really know this woman, can they? Wouldn't it be true to say, "Well, we haven't really met properly, have we?"

I'm pausing the film on purpose at this point to invite us to think about The Wicked Witch. There's no point in waiting for a scene where we get to know her story or her heart's desire. That just never happens. We do know she craves unlimited power and would use it to dominate everyone around her. She'd kill anyone who gets in her way. So how could you possibly get to know someone like her?

In the short term, you can't.

When I was little I loved my record player, an RCA Victrola. I had one 45-rpm record of songs from "Peter Pan." Maybe you know the song, "Never Smile at a Crocodile." Here's how it goes:

"Never smile at a crocodile,

No, you can't get friendly with a crocodile.

Don't be taken in by his welcome grin,

He's just tryin' to see how well you'll fit

Within his chin."

109

In Oz, The Wicked Witch intends evil in every scene. It is never safe to try to befriend her.

In the story, the character of The Wicked Witch originated with Dorothy's Kansas neighbor, Miss Gulch. As Miss Gulch is seizing Toto to have him destroyed, Dorothy calls her a *"wicked old witch."* I wonder if they ever met properly.

It seems unlikely. As the story opens Dorothy complains that Miss Gulch has just hit Toto, *"right over the back with a rake — just because she says he gets in her garden and chases her nasty old cat every day!"* Maybe Almira Gulch loves her garden and her cat and isn't rotten to the core. Maybe she and Dorothy have at least one thing in common: They each love their pets.

"Oh, but he doesn't do it every day — just once or twice a week — and he can't catch her old cat anyway." Just for the record, Dorothy doesn't seem bothered that her dog annoys this woman, trespassing into her garden *"just once or twice a week."* How would that sound in court?

And it could have come to that. But Toto gets no day in court. Instead the sheriff is summoned and things go from bad to worse. Miss Gulch appears at the Gale farm as judge, jury and executioner. She claims she's, *"all but lame from the bite on my leg,"* though she seemed to have no trouble peddling that bicycle of hers. *"That dog's a menace to the community. I'm taking him to the sheriff and make sure he's destroyed."*

Our Miss Gulch has gone nuclear.

Dorothy tries to take responsibility, better late than never: *"Please, Aunt Em! Toto didn't mean to. He didn't know he was doing anything wrong. I'm the one who ought to be punished. I let him go in her garden … you can send me to bed without supper…."*

Miss Gulch threatens, *"If you don't hand over that dog, I'll bring a damage suit that'll take your whole farm."* Aunt Em counters with a reasonable alternative: *"How would it be if she keeps him tied up? He's really gentle — with gentle people, that is."* Aunt Em utters that last line with the beginnings of contempt.

Miss Gulch will have none of it. *"I've got a notice! Let me have him!"*

Dorothy sobs, running from the room.

The screenplay reads, "Aunt Em stands looking at Miss Gulch with an expression of repressed anger." There's something to be said for repressed anger. It beats road rage, doesn't it?

Em continues, *"Almira Gulch … just because you own half the county doesn't mean you have the power to run the rest of us! For twenty-three years I've been dying to tell you what I thought of you … and now … well — being a Christian woman — I can't say it!"* She runs off, but not to comfort Dorothy. She's just too angry for words.

So, we haven't really met properly, have we?

I read this story through the lens of my Catholic Christian consciousness. Here's the question I have: How do we act toward those we want to label "wicked?" What do I do when I think I have an enemy who is evil to the core?

How did Jesus answer this question?

"Love your enemies. Pray for your persecutors." (Matthew 5:44-45)

"Do not return evil for evil." (Matthew 5:39)

Who would you say is humanity's most bitter enemy? The Christian tradition would say: Satan, the Father of Lies, the Prince of Darkness.

I was trained in the theology of Saint Thomas Aquinas. He contended that no one is purely evil, because God created only good. Therefore Satan has at least one good quality left. And what would that be? He's God's child, made in God's image. God is love, and God still loves Satan!

I spent five years studying theology and that's the most important thing I ever learned. Any time I might want to label someone a wicked witch, a crocodile or the spawn of Satan, like Auntie Em, being a Christian man ... I can't say it. I won't say it, because it isn't true. I may not be able to see the good in a particular person, but I believe in many things I can't see.

Living out the conviction that everyone deserves respect whether he or she behaves respectfully or not isn't easy. Loving an enemy is a spiritual discipline that requires stubborn persistence and God's help. I'm convinced it's worth the effort. In real life it's often done imperfectly ... two steps forward and one step back.

In the film, have you noticed that no one hates The Wicked Witch? No one plots revenge on her. They avoid her whenever possible. Instead, Dorothy, Scarecrow, Tin Man and Lion stay focused on their journey and on serving each other. And it's important that they do. Dorothy had warned Scarecrow as he was deciding to become her companion, *"Maybe you better not. I've got a witch mad at me, and you might get into trouble."*

"We've come such a long way already," Dorothy says a little farther down the road. *"You call that long? Why you've just begun,"* mocked The Wicked Witch. She isn't done with them yet. She'll loom larger the closer they get to the Emerald City. And now it's just over the horizon.

CHAPTER 17

Sleeping and Waking, Dying and Rising

Do you believe you will survive your death?

I ask people that question all the time. Much of my time is spent with church-going Christian people. Our greatest feast is Easter, when Jesus is risen from the dead. As nice as that is for him, he is called the "first fruits"; the rest of humanity will also rise again, each in our own time.

I don't think of this as just a religious belief, but a law of nature. I think it's a physics thing. You and I are each a bundle of energy. And energy can't be destroyed, only transferred. I believe that all human persons are eternal from the moment we come into being. We're mortal, yes, but immortal, too.

To believe otherwise, it follows that the life-and-death struggle of our existence is always won, in the end, by death. Death conquers. Death calls the shots. Death rules.

I'm always saddened when I read obituaries that say "so-and-so" lost her courageous battle with cancer. So, the last thing so-and-so was, was a loser. I'd rather not be defined by death, or be called a loser. Couldn't we say so-and-so crowned her life by living it courageously to her last breath? At checkers, when you get all the way to the other side of the board, your opponent must crown you, making you more mobile and powerful than ever before. I think that's what the day after your death will be like. If you doubt what I say is true, I look forward to meeting up with you after we've both made our journeys. I promise not to say, "I told you so." Nobody likes a cosmic smart aleck. But I believe you and I are in for many wonderful surprises.

As the Yellow Brick Road leads our travelers from darkness to light, we meet The Wicked Witch again, this time in her dark tower room. Her domain is the western sky, that place of the setting sun, the daily dying of the light. She has skirmished with Dorothy and company several times now. *"So you won't take warning, eh?"* she snarls at the image of the happy travelers in her crystal ball. *"All the worse for you, then — I'll take care of you now instead of later."* She's on the warpath.

The Wicked Witch concocts a chemical weapon… *"something with poison in it, I think, but attractive to the eye and soothing to the smell! Poppies … poppies … poppies will put them to sleep."* She runs her green fingers over the crystal ball, casting the spell. *"Now they'll sleep."*

The field of blood-red poppies is seen first in the crystal ball, then as a mine-field the travelers will enter unawares.

"There's Emerald City!" Dorothy points excitedly. *"Oh, we're almost there at last! At last!"*

And they run into the poppy field.

Poppies, from ancient times, have been associated with sleep and death. They're found on tombstones as a symbol of eternal sleep. The sleep The Wicked Witch is inducing is not a nap or an eight-hour rest. She doesn't want merely to delay them. She wants to stop them. Dead.

The Witch's poison must be airborne and inhaled, for all of the breathing members of the party to fall victim to it. The Tin Man and Scarecrow, neither of whom have need of breath, are unaffected. Toto is the first to succumb.

"Oh … oh, what's happening? What is it? I can't run anymore … I'm so sleepy. Please — I have to rest for just a minute." Dorothy falls to the ground and falls asleep.

"Comin' to think of it forty winks wouldn't be bad…" The Lion adds, yawning and keeling over.

The Scarecrow and Tin Man are powerless. They try to move Dorothy, but she's dead weight.

"Uh! Oh, this is terrible! Can't budge her an inch," says The Scarecrow. Again the Brainless One has a brainstorm: *"This is a spell, this is!"*

"It's the Wicked Witch!" says The Tin Man.

Toto, my Christ figure, remember, lies in eternal sleep. Companions Dorothy and Lion do too, with friend Scarecrow and Tin Man left to cry and cry out.

"HELP! HELP!" shouts The Tin Man.

"It's no use screaming at a time like this! Nobody will hear you!" replies The Scarecrow, who then adds his voice to the anguished prayer. *"HELP! HELP! HELP!"*

Lots of people want to believe in a listening God who hears their prayers, but are unsure that their prayers matter at all, especially in life-and-death situations.

Floating above the scene, Glinda appears, though Tin Man and Scarecrow are unaware of her. As she waves her wand, snowflakes begin falling gently upon the poppies.

"HELP! HELP! HELP!" The Scarecrow beseeches. Looking up in wonder he says, "It's snowing!"

Snow begins settling upon Dorothy, Toto and Lion.

"Oh, maybe that'll help! Oh, but it couldn't help!" says The Scarecrow.

And here I think he speaks for so many … the "spiritual but not religious," the ones for whom prayer is infrequent and expressed not in memorized words but from the heart. He says the only word that really needs to be said, with powerful love for his friends, giving it life: *"HELP!"*

Dorothy, "stirs slightly and opens her eyes," the screenplay reads. Rising, she points to The Tin Man, now rusted from crying.

"Oh, give me the oil can, quick!" Dorothy commands, for there's more life-saving work to be done. Soon she and Scarecrow are anointing him as we saw them do earlier in the forest.

Meanwhile The Lion and Toto awaken and rise, foiling The Wicked Witch. In her crystal ball she sees her defeat. Furious, she shrieks, *"Curse it! Curse it! Somebody always helps that girl! But shoes or no shoes ... I'm still great enough to conquer her! And woe to those who try to stop me!"*

Death doesn't go quietly. The Wicked Witch, until now, had only wanted the ruby slippers and the powers that came with them. She was more or less indifferent about Dorothy. But not anymore. Now she wants conquest.

Our friends are not thinking of death or threats. Their hearts are set on the gifts they desire and upon helping each other get to Emerald City to see the giver of all good gifts, the Wonderful Wizard of Oz.

They see the glistening city. When they first laid eyes on it, Dorothy gushed, *"It's beautiful, isn't it? Just like I knew it would be! He really must be a wonderful Wizard to live in a city like that!"* Now they leave the poppy field behind without a care in the world.

"Come on, let's get out of here. Look — Emerald City is closer and prettier than ever!" Dorothy cries.

I believe that, on the day of our death, we'll all hear words like that spoken by someone we love and who has gone on before us. Someone we love will be heaven-sent with this message: "Come on, let's get out of here." When we leave our death scenes behind we'll have loving companions old and new to go with us on the next step of our journey. And we'll be shown a vision of our own heart's desire, now closer and prettier than ever.

"They link arms and tramp out of the snow-covered field as they hear a chorus of voices off-screen begin to sing," the screenplay reads. It sounds like choirs of angels, I think, who sing:

"You're out of the woods
You're out of the dark
You're out of the night

Step into the sun
Step into the light..."

For there's more life to be lived. And there always will be.

CHAPTER 18

The Title Character

Soon the travelers will enter what the

screenplay calls, "a huge lofty hall, beautifully decorated in green and silver glass. At the far end is a short flight of stairs leading to a huge throne. On the steps are two silver urns, from which flames and smoke arise. A gigantic, shadowy head hovers over the throne."

A terrifying voice booms: *"Who are you?"*

The others shove Dorothy forward, making her their spokesperson.

"WHO ARE YOU?" the voice booms again.

Much later, with the trophy witch's broom in hand, the group will be back in this room to claim their promised gifts. As Toto unmasks that man behind the curtain, Dorothy will be the one asking the questions. She won't need to shout, for he'll find the simple, direct question terrifying enough: "Who are you?"

It's a question that deserves an answer. So, who is the story's title character?

We've met Miss Gulch, Dorothy, Toto, Auntie Em and Uncle Henry. We've met the farmhands, Hunk, Hickory and Zeke. And we've met the Witch of the North, Glinda the Good. Of all the story's main characters there is only one who is never known by a proper name, either in Kansas or in Oz. In Kansas he was the old carnival fakir, Professor Marvel. In Emerald City he's known as "The Wonderful Wizard of Oz." Whoever he is, this person is always subsumed under a role. The ancient Greeks had a word for that — *hypocrite*, which means "actor."

The guy in Kansas is someone acting like he can read your future in his crystal ball or introduce you to the crowned heads of Europe. In Emerald City he'll act like he can grant your every wish. But underneath the mask, or out from behind the curtain, who is this man?

I have a copy of a great old recording. It's an NBC Radio program called "Maxwell House Good News," which aired on June 29, 1939. The cast members of the MGM movie appear to promote the soon-to-be-released epic *The Wizard of Oz*. Frank Morgan, who plays The Wizard, appears on the show, in character. The announcer describes him as "that lovable humbug, that man with a power complex, in short, a delightful phony."

I like that description very much, because I think that is what author Frank Baum intended. He has created a hypocritical character who we cannot despise because there is a little of him in all of us.

The Wizard takes on a God-like role — hypocrisy on a cosmic scale. He lives in this temple-city. His own palace resembles a Gothic cathedral, huge green arches emphasizing the grandeur of the one who dwells there and, in this case, the insignificance of any visitor.

But just try to get into the place. It's no easy task. And no wonder, for this humbug must not be found out, or the show's over. The same character wears many disguises. He's the angry doorman at the city gate, then the cabby who diverts the travelers, taking them not to The Wizard, but to a beauty parlor. Later, he's the palace guard who bellows, *"Nobody can see the great Oz, not nobody, not nohow!"* Finally, he's the manipulator, at first unseen, who projects the scowling, disembodied head of The Wizard of Oz onto the back wall of the inner sanctum surrounded by hellfire and smoke.

"Hypocrite" is a word I seldom use. It's usually spoken in judgment and, most often, unkindly. We can be especially quick to use it to describe people we've never met, like powerful political, business or religious leaders. Its indictment is too brutal for face-to-face conversation.

Sometimes people who have no use for organized religion will announce, "I don't need to go to church. It's just full of hypocrites!" I tell them, politely, "Well, we're usually not that full. We'll all scoot over and make room for you."

It's at his moment of unmasking, when Toto peels back the curtain, that we learn anything about the real person at the center of this story. It's Dorothy who asks the question that gets to the heart of the matter: *Who are you?*

His reply is half-amplified, half-whimpered. *"I AM THE GREAT AND POWERFUL … wizard of oz."*

The Scarecrow calls him a humbug, and The Lion and Tin Man agree.

"Yes, that is exactly so. I'm a humbug," The Wizard replies.

"Oh, you're a very bad man!" Dorothy scolds. And in one of the most profound lines of the film, The Wizard replies, *"Oh, no, my dear, I — I'm a very good man — I'm just a very bad wizard."*

What about you? Have you ever been tempted to pretend to be what you are not? That doesn't make you a bad person. But you might be a very bad wizard.

With that illusion shattered, The Wizard must face the travelers who are now demanding the gifts he'd promised them. And here The Wizard's wise humanity shines through. He knows they already possess what they seek, and he says so.

The Scarecrow has all the brains he needs, *"But,"* The Wizard says, *"there's one thing you haven't got! A diploma!"* And of course he confers one.

As for courage, The Lion has it already, *"But one thing you haven't got! A medal!"* He pins it on.

And a heart? The Tin Man just needs a simple testimonial, *"... a token of our esteem and affection."* Please accept this heart-shaped clock. It ticks.

Toto, remember, hasn't asked for a thing. He hasn't pretended or aspired to be anything he is not. He has been and is still completely at home being a loving companion and friend. In that way I think he's truly Godly.

But Dorothy. *"Yes, what about Dorothy?"* Tin Man asks.

Can The Wizard get her back to Kansas? Not really, but slipping back into character he acts like he can. Dorothy even asks, *"Oh, but are you a clever enough wizard to manage it?"*

"Child, you cut me to the quick!" He reverts to his carnival blather. As he does, we hear a very little bit of personal biography seeping through. His carnival balloon had been blown off course and floated into Emerald City. He was instantly acclaimed, *"Oz, the First Wizard de luxe!"* He laughs, adding, *"Times being what they were, I accepted the job."*

It was as simple as that.

He acted from his own humanity long enough to bestow the gifts, but then floats back into a character he's pretended to be for so long that it's almost second nature. He's just a guy on an incomplete journey, like everybody else. But he's well-meaning — a lovable humbug and delightful phony — now hustling Dorothy, and Toto, into a balloon he says is bound for Kansas, but that he doesn't know how to steer.

Thank God, Toto leaps out just in time and Dorothy follows. The Wizard — whoever he is — floats away without them.

"Oh! Come back, come back — don't go without me! Please come back!" Dorothy screams.

The Wizard, ever the actor, mutters to himself, "*...Ruined my exit!*" Quickly, he recovers.

"Good-bye, folks," he shouts waving to his adoring audience.

"Good-bye! Good-bye! Good-bye!"

But he doesn't just disappear from the view of the townsfolk. Before that can happen he's already out of focus to himself. He disappears in plain sight, but not by magic. He loses sight of himself and disappears under a role. While looking in a mirror try asking yourself if he reminds you of anyone you know.

CHAPTER 19

Pilgrims

I paused the film to spend a few moments considering the title character, the person who is the purpose of our travelers' journeys — The Wizard of Oz. As we rejoin them on their journey they're crossing the poppy field and leaving the eerie forest behind. They can see the Emerald City rising up before them.

Have you ever been on a pilgrimage, a journey that made you a pilgrim? A pilgrim is literally "one who is far afield." It's related to the word "acre." A pilgrim is not merely a tourist who vacations in a distant place and who brings home photos and souvenirs. A pilgrim sojourns with an open heart, ready to be changed by the experience. Going off one's familiar turf, in search of something deeper and truer, this is the journey of a pilgrim.

A pilgrimage might be religious. For Jews, Jerusalem, and for Muslims, Mecca, may be pilgrimage destinations. Christians may travel to sites associated with Jesus or one of the saints. Secular shrines attract those with deep affection for music, sports or history. Battlefields and cemeteries may inspire a deeper patriotism, love of one's fatherland.

If you went on a pilgrimage, where would you go? What would you seek?

Dorothy, Scarecrow, Tin Man and Lion each set out on a quest, seeking their heart's desire. The Wizard of Oz, they were told, would supply all they desired. *"Look, Emerald City is closer and prettier than ever!"* Dorothy cries. "They link arms and tramp out of the snow-covered field," the screenplay reads. That linking reminds me of "religare," Latin for "bind together." Religion and ligament derive from this word. Many seekers opt to bind themselves together, like mountain climbers scaling a peak.

An unseen angelic chorus begins to sing. The screenplay simply calls them "Optimistic Voices." The pilgrims hear them, looking up and around, then skipping toward the city.

"You're out of the woods
You're out of the dark
You're out of the night
Step into the sun
Step into the light
Keep straight ahead for
The most glorious place
On the face
Of the earth or the sky."

The Book of Psalms is lyric poetry considered sacred to Jews and Christians. Some of the psalms were sung by pilgrimage groups joyous at their ascent to the Jerusalem temple:

"I was glad when I heard them say,
"Let us go up to the house of the Lord."
Psalm 122:1

The singing continues:

"Hold onto your breath

Hold onto your heart

Hold onto your hope

March up to the gate

And bid it open—"

"Enter his gates with thanksgiving."

Psalm 100:4-5

The scene shifts momentarily to The Witch's Castle. Grabbing her broomstick, The Wicked Witch flies through the window, shrieking, *"To the Emerald City as fast as lightning!"* But this moment belongs to the pilgrims, now at the city's gate.

Dorothy rings the bell and a little window in the door opens.

We'll meet five guises of Professor Marvel here: first the doorman, then the cabby, the guard, and two faces of The Wizard of Oz. Formidable Emerald City is really a house of cards, but that's not evident yet. Each time the pilgrims try to advance they'll be met with resistance.

"Who rang that bell?" the doorman shouts fiercely.

"We did!" the pilgrims reply.

"Can't you read?" the doorman shouts still more fiercely.

"Read what?" asks The Scarecrow.

"The notice!"

"What notice?"

"It's on the door — as plain as the nose on your face! It's ah — oh-oh-oh-oh."

He slams the door shut.

This is not going so well, is it? In church culture one sometimes encounters attack receptionists whose mission seems to be keeping parishioners away from the pastor.

They read the card just placed on the door: *"Bell out of order. Please knock."*

So Dorothy knocks.

"Ask, and it will be given to you. Seek and you will find; knock and it will be opened to you. For everyone who asks receives, the one who seeks finds, and to the one who knocks it will be opened." (Matthew 7:7-8)

"Well, that's more like it! Now, state your business."

"We want to see the Wizard!"

The Doorman, so shocked he almost falls, says, *"The Wizard? Ah — but nobody can see the Great Oz! Nobody's ever seen the Great Oz! Even I've never seen him!"*

I love this next part.

The screenplay notes have Dorothy ask, guilelessly, *"Well, then, how do you know there is one?"*

What Sunday school pupil hasn't asked a "God question" the teacher couldn't answer?

"Because — he ... ah ... b — I — oh —."

Unable to think of a good reason, the Doorman shouts with aggravation, *"You're wasting my time!"*

But Dorothy stays focused. *"Oh, please — please, sir — I've got to see the Wizard."* Then she name-drops to try to get past this bouncer. *"The Good Witch of the North sent me."*

"Prove it!" the doorman barks.

"She's wearing the ruby slippers she gave her!" The Scarecrow announces. The slippers get a closeup.

"Oh, so she is! Why didn't you say that in the first place? Come on in!"

Why is that "a horse of a different color" to this sham wizard? Because he's insecure. Most of us are in one way or another. There are powers all around him he can't control. There are witches with real power and, now even a little girl with magical shoes.

"Come on in!" he says.

"I rejoiced when I heard them say,

Let us go into the House of the Lord.

For now our feet are standing

within your gates, Oh, Jerusalem."

Psalm 122:1

The pilgrims enter the city with its glittering streets, and are greeted immediately by a cockney cabdriver, another Professor Marvel disguise.

"Cabby! Cabby! Just what you're looking for! Tyke you anywhere in the city we does!"

"Well, would you take us to see The Wizard?" Dorothy asks.

"The Wizard? The Wizard? ... I ... can' t...well, yes, of course.... But first I'll tyke you to a little place where you can tidy up a bit."

And before you know it, they're at the entrance to the "Wash & Brush Up Co."

Are you familiar with the Catholic idea of purgatory? It's not actually a doctrine or dogma of the church. It's more of a working hypothesis about where the soul goes first after death on its way to heaven. Purge just means to cleanse thoroughly. Instead of metaphysical flames, Oz has customized spas. After the wearying journey, the pilgrims are pampered with spa treatments. If heaven has any need of a purgatorial antechamber, I think Oz's spa would be a nice touch.

The pilgrims, now looking their best, join the citizens of Emerald City in the city square. They're laughing the day away in the Merry Old Land of Oz. There are many ha-ha-has and ho-ho-hos, and joy all around. As the laughter crescendos the pilgrims break into the first few bars of the marching song, "We're Off to See the Wizard." Suddenly, a loud noise booms overhead. Ominous music and The Witch's shrieking laughter silences the crowd. The Witch is writing something in the sky.

"SURRENDER DOROTHY"

136

The Witch's lack of punctuation leaves the message ambiguous. Is it addressed to Dorothy? "Surrender, Dorothy!" Or is it a command to The Wizard and the populace? "Surrender Dorothy."

"Dorothy? Who's Dorothy?" someone asks.

"The Wizard will explain it!" answers another.

And before you know it all these sheep without a shepherd are rushing to The Wizard's palace.

"Dear, whatever shall we do?" Dorothy asks, obviously shaken.

"Well, we'd better hurry if we're going to see the Wizard!" says The Scarecrow.

The mob has barely assembled at the palace door when the guard, Professor Marvel again, bellows:

"Here — here! Here! Everything is all right. Stop that now — just — every — it's all right! Everything is all right! The Great and Powerful Oz has got matters well in hand — I hope — so you can all go home! And there's nothing to worry about! Get out of here now — go on! Go on home, and I — I — go home."

Of course, going home is exactly what Dorothy wants to do. It's just not as easy as it sounds. But the pilgrims press on to the front of the now retreating mob.

"If you please, sir," Dorothy persists, *"we want to see The Wizard right away — all four of us!"* She's not counting Toto at the moment.

"Orders are, nobody can see the Great Oz, not nobody, not nohow!"

Undaunted, The Scarecrow adds a very important piece of information: *"But she's Dorothy!"*

"The Witch's Dorothy? Humph! Well, that makes a difference! Just wait here — I'll announce you at once!"

Dorothy was made aware long ago that she'd made a powerful enemy of The Wicked Witch. Power of one kind or another surrounds this girl. Professor Marvel forfeited home and was seduced by power long ago. He has to risk letting her and her companions in. Under the guise of the guard he marches inside.

And so it looks like Dorothy, Scarecrow, Tin Man, Lion and Toto have reached their destination, the end of their pilgrimage, the rainbow's end. Soon they'll be face to face with The Wizard, The Wonderful Wizard of Oz.

CHAPTER 20

If I Were King

"Just wait here — I'll announce you at once."

The guard has marched inside to arrange their audience with the Great and Powerful Oz. Earlier, Dorothy sang of a place where *"the dreams that you dare to dream really do come true."* They believe they have arrived at that place.

"Did you hear that? He'll announce us at once! I've as good as got my brain!" says The Scarecrow.

"I can fairly hear my heart beating!" adds The Tin Man.

"I'll be home in time for supper!" cries Dorothy.

"In another hour I'll be King of the Forest. Long live the King!" says The Lion, feeling a song coming on.

The song of The Cowardly Lion is one of the most beloved scenes in *The Wizard of Oz*. The Lion, like all of us, is a work in progress. His dream, the way he imagines it, is a mixture of immature egoism and profundity. He wants to be respected — literally to be given a second look. Who doesn't? He wants others to see value and valor in him. He wants to rule over his subjects, but with compassion for the weak. And he knows none of it will happen without the gift of *courage*.

The Lion might not have courage yet, but he does possess one treasure: good friends. Many of the dreams that we dare to dream remain hidden and unexpressed, for fear we'd be laughed at if we ever voiced them. Friends who reverence us reverence our dreams, even dreams not yet fully dreamt. The Lion opens his heart. That requires courage. And remember, *cor*, Latin for heart, is the root of the word courage. He bursts into song:

"If I were King of the Forest,

Not Queen, not Duke, not Prince.

My regal robes of the forest

Would be satin, not cotton, not chintz.

I'd command each thing, be it fish or fowl,

With a woof, and a woof, and a royal growl—woof.

As I'd click my heel,

All the trees would kneel,

And the mountains bow,

And the bulls kowtow,

And the sparrow would take wing

'F—I…'f…I…were King."

Many cultures have conflated kingship and divinity. The Caesars of Rome were gods. The divine right of kings assumes that the king's status is ordained by God and the king's will is an extension of God's will. The Lion's dream of kingship includes some of these elements.

"As I'd click my heel,

All the trees would kneel,

And the mountains bow,"

The Hebrew prophet Isaiah wrote of the coming of a universal king:

"For you will go out with joy

And be led forth with peace;

The mountains and hills will break forth

Into shouts of joy before you.

And the trees of the field will clap their hands."

Isaiah 55:12

It's heady stuff having chipmunks genuflect to you, and hearing a band strike up "Hail to the Chief" every time you enter a room. At first, even the upgrade in wardrobe is alluring:

"My regal robes of the forest,

Will be satin, not cotton, not chintz."

Jesus spoke about a leader, John the Baptist, who wore only crude camel's hair.

"But what did you go out to see? A man dressed in soft clothing?

Those who wear soft clothing are in kings' palaces."

Matthew 11:8

"Among those born of women there has not arisen anyone greater than he.

Yet the one who is least in the kingdom of heaven is greater than he."

Matthew 11:11

"Beware those who like to go about in long robes and love salutations in the marketplace and the best seats in the synagogue."
Mark 12:38-39

I think of that as I don the priestly robes before I say Mass and make my way down the aisle to the presider's chair in front, especially amid the splendor of Stanford's Memorial Church.

But there is a grace note in The Lion's song:

"Though my tail would lash,
I would show compash
For every underling,
'F—I…'f…I…were King---
Just King."

As The Lion grows into his heart — his *cor* — and finds his courage, I think his fascination with fine garments will wane. For he has a compassionate heart for those who are suffering and who have less power than he. Isn't that a quality we want in our leaders? There's a phrase to describe such leaders: public servants.

"You know how the kings of the nations lord it over them?" Jesus asked.
"Their great ones make their importance felt. It cannot be that way with you.

The one who is greatest among you must become like the least, and the leader like the servant."

Luke 22: 25-26

I've met many people who've chosen lives of servant leadership, many inspired by the example of President John F. Kennedy. His words still inspire: "Ask not what your country can do for you, but what you can do for your country."

One future day, The Wizard of Oz will publicly pass his throne on to a triumvirate of rulers:

"I hereby decree that until what time — if any — that I return, The Scarecrow by virtue of his highly superior brains, shall rule in my stead, assisted by The Tin Man, by virtue of his magnificent heart, and The Lion, by virtue of his courage! Obey them as you would me!"

But first The Lion must find his courage. He'll fear nothing — not a rhinoceros, hippopotamus or an elephant.

"What if it were a brontosaurus?" The Scarecrow wonders.

"I'd show him who was King of the Fores'." The Lion answers.

"How?"

The Lion begins to be lionhearted. He delivers this speech in praise of his prized virtue:

"How?…Courage!

What makes a king out of a slave!

…Courage!

What makes the flag on a mast to wave!

…Courage!

What makes the elephant charge his tusk

In the misty mist or the dusky dusk?

What makes the muskrat guard his musk?

…Courage!

What make the sphinx the seventh wonder?

…Courage!

What makes the dawn come up like thunder?

…Courage!

What makes the Hottentot so hot?

What puts the 'ape' in apricot?

What have they got that I ain't got?"

"Courage!" the others cry in unison.

"You can say that again! Ha, ha — huh?"

What The Lion has plenty of at the moment is the bane of his existence: cowardice. *"Well, wouldn't you be degraded to be seen in the company of a cowardly lion?"* he'd asked, sobbing, when the others invited him to join them on their journey. *"I would."*

When I looked for the root of the word *cowardice* I could hardly believe what I found. It comes from the Latin *coe* and the Old French *coart*, which means tail! It seems that centuries ago people witnessed cowardly behavior in animals that cowered in fear with their tail between their legs. The expression "to turn tail" describes fleeing in fear.

The Lion's tail gets a mention in his anthem:

"Though my tail would lash
I would show compash
To every underling."

He's beginning to imagine combining a courageous disposition with a gentle heart.

Soon the travelers will be walking together down a long, vaulted corridor in Oz's palace. Lion, stopping, whimpers, *"Wait a minute, fellas! I was just thinkin'*
— I really don't want to see The Wizard this much. I better wait for you outside." He turns to go, but they stop him.

"What's the matter?" The Scarecrow asks.

"Oh he's just ascared again," replies The Tin Man.

Dorothy tries to reassure him, *"Don't you know the Wizard's going to give you some courage?"*

Twiddling his tail nervously and wiping away tears with the brush on the end, he bawls, *"I'd be too afraid to ask him for it!"*

"Oh, well, then we'll ask him for you!" Dorothy offers.

He's not buying it. *"I'd sooner wait outside."* He turns to run, but they stop him.

"Why? Why?" Dorothy asks.

"Because I'm still scared!" The Lion sobs.

"Come on," Dorothy encourages.

Suddenly The Lion howls in pain. *"Somebody pulled my tail!"*

"You did it yourself!" The Scarecrow replies.

" I — oh — ," The Lion groans. And they join hands, to give him courage.

Later Dorothy is trapped in The Witch's castle, in need of rescue. They must climb a dark, slippery mountain to reach her. Who leads the way? The Lion — with The Tin Man clinging to his tail.

"I - I - I hope my strength holds out," The Lion stammers.

"I hope your tail holds out! Oh!" The Tin Man cries, losing his footing.

Finally, after overpowering three Winkie Guards, Scarecrow, Tin Man and Lion put on their military uniforms and fall in line as the guards goose-step their way into the castle. The screenplay notes that, "the last one is The Lion, who is having a dreadful time with his tail." Which is wagging this way and that, sticking out from beneath the hem of the uniform coat. His tail is definitely not tucked between his legs now.

"What have they got that I ain't got?" The Lion's song concludes.

"Courage!" his friends reply.

But, remember, there is a place where the dreams that you dare to dream really do come true. It's here and it's now. The Lion is growing in courage bit by bit.

The camera pans to the palace door. The guard emerges.

"Ahhhhh! The Wizard says go away!"

He exits, slamming the door behind him.

CHAPTER 21

CAUTION

I have a small office in my home. It's full of

Wizard of Oz collectibles given me by family and friends over the years. On the door hangs a sign confronting any potential visitor:

NOBODY GETS IN TO SEE THE WIZARD!

NOT NOBODY! NOT NOHOW!

For most of my childhood there was a sign on my mom and dad's bedroom door. It was just one word:

CAUTION.

Here's how it got there. My dad was Captain Max Castle. He was a harbor pilot who steered huge ships and docked them in tight places. Often the cargo was gasoline. The next ship over might be full of molten sulfur, the stuff they put on the head of a match. His job was stressful. He had to work for as long as the job took and grab some sleep whenever he could, day or night. The prime directive around our house was "Don't wake up Daddy."

One day my little brother, Mike, and I were playing in the dirt beneath Dad's bedroom window. I was about 6 years old; Mike was 4. For Christmas we'd gotten a set of little road signs to use with our cars and trucks. There were stop signs and curve signs and railroad crossing signs. Our roads and bridges were constantly under repair and the drivers of the cars in our little world often sped off mountainsides plunging to horrible deaths. One sign in particular might have saved some of

151

their lives. It just read: CAUTION. It had hard plastic legs on either end. It was a great sign.

This day Mike and I both wanted the CAUTION sign at the same time. First there was some grabbing and pushing, then some dirt throwing, and finally, shouting.

At the height of the conflict there was a whooshing sound above us as the bedroom window opened and an angry voice boomed: "Boys, stay right there."

We woke up Daddy.

He was there in no time, in the backyard in his underwear, wanting to know what the fight that ruined his sleep was all about. The CAUTION sign. He didn't care who had it first or whose turn it was to use it. "Lemme have it," he said. He crouched down to our level, took the CAUTION sign and snapped its little legs off. The way he did it made me think he'd really like to have snapped our little legs off.

"Boys," he said, "Come with me."

He marched us up the long hall to his bedroom, and, taking some tape, stuck the sign on his bedroom door.

"Can you read that? What does it say?"

"It says CAUTION, Daddy."

Over the years the walls got fresh paint, old carpets were replaced, and we all grew older. But the CAUTION sign was always there on Daddy's door.

Back in the prologue I told you about the time I got so angry with him and imploded. I decided to close my heart to him, to run away without going anywhere. And how I almost succeeded at going off to college at his expense until something extraordinary happened. That religious retreat where I was filled with holy presence and power was called "The Happening." If it would help refresh your memory, you might want to pause here and reread the prologue.

So, now, fast-forward with me. I'm 18 now, finishing high school and about to leave home for college. I admit to a bunch of people on this retreat that I feel rotten about my relationship with my dad. I hadn't really spoken to him in years. But I didn't know what to do about it.

I got home from the retreat and sat on the edge of my bed. Dad was in the next room, asleep. I said a prayer and the palms of my hands heated up and started shaking. I felt full of power. I was being given the gift I needed to open my heart and find my voice ... the gift of courage.

I decided to wake up Daddy and initiate a father-son talk. I walked out into the hall and took a few steps toward his room. I couldn't do it. I turned around and went back into my room. To this day, when I watch the scene where they're all walking down Oz's scary hall approaching The Wizard, and The Lion turns tail and runs, I think of how I felt that day. Back in my room I had no peace. I knew I was afraid, but my parents hadn't raised a coward. I thought, "If I don't do this now, I never will."

So I went back down the hall to his door. I had forgotten about that CAUTION sign. It was right at eye level, staring me in the face. But I'd been too cautious for too long.

I knocked lightly on the door. I could hear him snoring. I've inherited that from my dad. I knocked a little louder, and then tried the knob. It was unlocked. I opened the door, stuck my head in, and whispered, "Dad, it's me."

Nothing.

So I walked over to the foot of the bed and said a little louder, "Dad, it's me."

Still nothing.

So I shook the mattress lightly. This was harder than I thought it would be. I moved farther up the mattress until I was standing over his head. I shook the mattress again.

He burst upright, shouting, his arms flailing. I felt like I'd woken a bear.

"It's just me, Dad. I need to talk to you and if I don't do it now I'll lose my nerve."

"Put on the lamp," he said, sitting up in bed. "OK," he said, "talk to me."

I took a deep breath.

"Did you know I stopped talking to you five years ago?"

What he said next completely threw me.

"Yep. I just didn't know what to do about it."

I was 18 years old and had been around him my entire life, and I had never heard him admit that he didn't know something.

"Well, I want to start over," I said. I told him about the report card incident, now years ago. He listened. When I was finished he asked, "Anything else?" Then I asked him a very blunt question: "Isn't it true that you love David more than me?"

He thought for a minute.

"Yep," he said. "That's true."

"Well, thanks for telling me the truth," I said. "It's always felt like that."

He tried to tell me about the bond between a father and his first-born son and that it was in the Bible. Here I thought he was out of his depth, trying to prove to his second son that this rank ordering was a law of the universe. It didn't matter that the words were difficult to hear or that his argumentation was kind of fumbling. I had just woken him from a deep sleep. And he was speaking the truth to me from his heart.

"I might be your second son, but I don't like to be referred to by number," I said without disrespect. He often introduced me that way. I remember him telling a salesman on the phone, "I'm gonna send my number two son to pick up those tires."

"You named me. From now on I'd like it if you would call me by my name."

"Fair enough," he said. "Anything else?"

"That's plenty for now," I said. "Thanks for listening to me."

"I love you, Dad," I said, for the first time.

"I love you, too, son."

We hugged awkwardly. I left, and he went back to sleep.

The years that followed were hard for him. He loved hard work. But his job was physically demanding. And he didn't age all that well. Then came big trouble: Parkinson's disease. It took him away by inches over about 10 years. He couldn't talk sensibly for much of the last three years, or at all for the last six months.

I'd visit and sit next to his bed, talking at him hoping something would be heard. Sometimes he'd just stare and I'd stare back. And I'd think of the day we both found our courage and began to find our way back home to one another. ❖

CHAPTER 22

Unholy
Encounter

"The Wizard says go away!"

the guard barks. Then he slams the door in their faces. These spiritual seekers have gone to so much trouble only to be denied access to The Wizard.

"Looks like we came a long way for nothing," The Scarecrow says, sadly.

Dorothy slumps to the ground. The screenplay notes that she's "losing her courage for the first time." Then she begins to cry.

Dorothy has landed on The Wizard's doorstep because she did as she was told. She could not return to Kansas the way she came. It was Glinda the Good Witch who pointed her toward the Emerald City and to The Wizard of Oz, who she said was *"very good, but very mysterious."*

But Dorothy hasn't always been the obedient good little girl. As her friends try to console her, her conscience accuses her: *"Auntie Em was so good to me, and I never appreciated it … running away and hurting her feelings. Professor Marvel said she was sick. She may be dying! And it's all my fault."* Here Dorothy is like the rest of us, some mixed-up mixture of virtue and vice trying to make her way through life … trying to find her way home. Her journey has brought her to the threshold of the house of the god of Oz, where she is turned away rudely.

This scene affects me deeply as a man who stands at the door of the sacred. I'm employed by the largest religious system on Earth, the Roman Catholic Church. Too often its representatives bar the door to keep out the riffraff, the sort of people Jesus notoriously hung out with.

The guard doesn't disappear, however. He peeps through a little window in the door he has just slammed, and hears Dorothy's lament. In spite of himself, he allows something holy to happen. Heart speaks to heart. He hears Dorothy's pain, and allows it to touch his own. He has compassion; he "suffers with." A flood of tears stream down his cheeks as Dorothy cries, *"I'll never forgive myself! Never-never-never!"* The guard sobs, *"Oh, Oh! Please don't cry anymore! I'll get you in to The Wizard somehow! Come on. I had an Aunt Em myself once."*

The guard disappears, as the doors of the palace slowly swing open. He can't accompany them because he must hurry away to assume another of his guises. He'll soon be pretending to be the great and powerful Wizard of Oz.

So the travelers must make their way unescorted down a long corridor, which the screenplay says, "seems to stretch on forever, high and narrow … with an awe-inspiring air of mystery and silence." It's a massive series of green lofted arches reminiscent of a Gothic cathedral. It points upward to a sky god, and The Wizard fits the type. He dropped from the sky in his carnival balloon. Later, when unmasked, he'll explain that he landed in, *"the heart of this noble city, where I was instantly acclaimed Oz, the First Wizard de luxe!"*

His palace doesn't facilitate a holy encounter, though. It's designed to do just the opposite. Remember what the guard had said earlier: *"Orders are: Nobody can see the Great Oz, not nobody, nohow!"* The corridor that leads to the inner sanctum inspires fear. The Cowardly Lion is shaken by it; he wants no part of it. *"Wait a minute, fellas! I was just thinkin' I really don't want to see The Wizard this much. I better wait for you outside."* He turns to go, but they stop him.

"Don't you know The Wizard's going to give you some courage?" Dorothy reassures him.

"I'd be too scared to ask him for it," The Lion replies, bursting into tears.

"Oh well, then we'll ask him for you!" Dorothy offers. The community makes up for the weakness of the individual member and carries him along. We can ask God for whatever we want for ourselves. But love makes us concerned about others. Lots of our prayers are for them.

"I'd sooner wait outside," The Lion frets. But the community knows his heart's desire and helps him seek it in spite of himself. They join hands. Prayerful communities do that.

Immense doors swing open, revealing a throne room. They walk cautiously forward. As they enter, a man's voice booms, *"Come forward!"* The voice doesn't invite — it commands. The lofty hall is dark. At the front are two silver urns belching flames and blood-red smoke. The rear wall is a triangle of cylinders like backlit organ pipes. Projected on them is the flickering image of an angry man's head — disembodied, disincarnate. It shouts at them, *"I am Oz, the Great and Powerful! Who are you?"*

He asks their names but doesn't want to know them at all. He will summon them forward, insult them and silence them when they try to tell their stories.

Dorothy steps forward as leader and spokesperson. She replies, *"I — if you please, I am Dorothy, the small and meek."* Here I'm reminded of the Sermon on the Mount in the fifth chapter of Matthew. It's Jesus' most beloved teaching: *"Blessed are the meek, for they shall inherit the earth."* Dorothy would happily settle for a tiny bit of it, back in Kansas. She tries to continue, *"We've come to ask you …."*

But Oz interrupts, screaming, *"SILENCE!"*

Dorothy runs back to join the others.

Sometimes, in the course of my ministry I have to ask for money from great and powerful — and wealthy — folks. I've been granted audience in the powerful corner office on the 30th floor. In what scary places has your life landed you?

"Step forward, Tin Man!"

He trembles so hard his joints rattle. Dorothy shoves him forward.

"You dare to come to me for a heart — do you?" Oz bellows. *"You clinking, clanking clattering collection of caliginous junk!"*

Tin Man tries to relate a story, but he, too, is silenced.

Next it's poor Scarecrow's turn.

"And you, Scarecrow, have the effrontery to ask for a brain? You billowing bale of bovine fodder!" Oz is big on alliterative insults.

The Scarecrow does what simple people do in the presence of their betters. He addresses Oz with puffery. *"Yes, your Honor — I mean, Your Excellency — I— I mean Your Wizardry!"* Here his lack of a spine serves him well. He's a pile of straw groveling before the throne.

"Enough!" shouts Oz as The Scarecrow stumbles backward.

"And you, Lion!" Oz booms. *"Well!"*

And The Lion faints, frightened to death.

Everything about this encounter has been unholy. Dorothy, angrily, says so.

"You ought to be ashamed of yourself! Frightening him like that, when he came to you for help!" But Oz isn't through.

"Silence, whippersnapper. The beneficent Oz has every intention of granting your requests!" But there will be a catch. A big one. *"But first you must prove yourself worthy by performing a very small task. Bring me the broomstick of The Wicked Witch of the West!"*

Here the heart of the matter is revealed. Oz the great, the powerful, the beneficent, is also Oz the fearful. Tyrants and bullies always are. Fear enthroned is far uglier than cowardice face-down on the floor.

"You know how the rulers of this world lord it over others?" Jesus asked. *"How their great ones make their importance felt? It must not be that way with you. The one who wants to be first must serve the others."*

The Wicked Witch would kill to get those powerful ruby slippers and The Wizard will try to turn innocent people into killers all for the sake of an enchanted broomstick. The Cowardly Lion sees where this is all heading and asks, *"But what if she kills us first?"*

Oz doesn't give a damn. *"I said GO,"* he blares.

Christian sanctuaries are dominated by our main symbol, the cross. Catholic churches often have a prominent crucifix — a cross bearing the completely powerless dead body of Jesus the God-man. The all-powerful One gives away all power. He's not a disembodied shouting head, but love incarnate, giving his life away for the sake of those he loves, whether they love him back or take his life. There is no transactional sham-religious bargaining here — I'll give you this if you give me that. That's all the weak and fearful Wizard of Oz is capable of at the moment. He'll betray those who sought his help in order to keep himself secure. It's an unholy encounter The Wizard has had with Dorothy, Tin Man, Scarecrow and Lion. So many people have had unholy encounters with someone who dwelt in the sanctuary.

Only one character came there needing nothing, asking nothing and desiring nothing more than to be the faithful companion on the journey, even in the face of death: love incarnate, Toto.

CHAPTER 23

Regathering

Remember when Dorothy, Toto and Scarecrow were befriending The Tin Man?

He felt worthless. He called himself "an empty kettle" because he had no heart. When Dorothy invited him on the journey to ask The Wizard of Oz for one, Tin Man considered an important, if depressing, possibility: *"Well, suppose The Wizard wouldn't give me one when we got there?"* After adding The Lion to their company they sang about how good life would be once they've received their gifts. It was Dorothy who added a big "if": *"If the Wizard is a wizard who will serve."*

As it has turned out so far, he won't give them what they seek. He wants to be served rather than to serve. *"The beneficent Oz has every intention of granting your requests,"* he said to those he'd just insulted and scared half to death. *"First you must prove yourself worthy by performing a very small task. Bring me the broomstick of The Wicked Witch of the West."* The Wizard has been called "wonderful" in song, time and again, *"becoz of the wonderful things he does."* We haven't seen that yet from him, have we?

This part of the story saddens me the most. Sincere, wounded folks, who've been trying their best, ask this God figure for what they long for most, only to have their whole quest turned into an ugly business transaction. They came asking for gifts knowing they had nothing of equal value to offer in return. Their intention was to "pay it forward" in generous service to others. But they don't find unconditional love, acceptance or even courtesy in The Wizard's presence. They find something very different: a relationship built on conditions. For performing what is not at all what he calls, *"a very small task,"* he promises to grant their requests. Even if he is true to his word, they won't really be gifts anymore, but commodities bought for a price. Instead of receiving their love, admiration and gratitude, The Wizard will receive what he wants even more, an instrument of abusive power: The Witch's broomstick.

Nevertheless, our friends regather themselves. And here they can teach us something, I think. Let's observe what they don't do:

They don't hate. Anybody. They don't curse The Wizard. They don't even have an unkind word for The Witch.

They don't moan about not getting what they asked for. They came asking for gifts. Gifts, by definition, are not entitlements. When they don't get the gifts they wanted, they don't behave like spoiled children the day after Christmas.

They don't blame others or each other.

And, most importantly, they don't give up. They don't quit.

Sometimes I feel way more than tired. Sometimes life gets hardest right when I feel like I've got nothing left to give. Sometimes I feel weary to my bones. That's how I see our travelers in this next part of their journey. They're up against bigger challenges than anything they've faced so far in lives that were difficult already. They can't change the circumstance they're in. They can only try to do their best within it.

Where do people with difficult lives and difficult current circumstances find the energy to keep going in a positive direction? First of all, they stay grounded in the present moment. Mulling over the past while spiritually depleted invites resentment and self-pity. Flying ill-prepared into a future featuring big challenges can be overwhelming and self-defeating. It's best to be still and take a deep breath. "Spirit" means breath. To seek inspiration means to breathe in. Deep breathing slows the pulse and calms the body. It brings peace.

There's a very popular prayer that's good for such a moment. I'm sure you've heard of "The Serenity Prayer." It begins like this:

God, grant me the serenity

to accept the things I cannot change;

courage to change the things I can,

and wisdom to know the difference.

This prayer, or any prayer for peace and wisdom, keeps me from going back into the fray feeling alone and resourceless.

Dorothy, Toto, Scarecrow, Tin Man and Lion have a new short-term goal that unites them. They'll pick each other up and literally put each other back together. They'll encourage each other. It will take every act of love and service they can muster to get that broomstick and deliver it to The Wizard.

The next scene opens on a sign that announces:

HAUNTED FOREST

WITCHES CASTLE

1 MILE.

Below is some well-meaning advice: "I'd turn back if I were you." The Lion reads it first and turns around to start back. We've probably all turned back a time or two, because we were afraid. But there are moments of truth that call for us to press on. Luckily, The Lion has his friends. Scarecrow and Tin Man link arms with him and turn him back around. He's not grateful at the moment. He growls at them, crying, his legs pedaling wildly in the air. Still, he let's himself be carried forward by their encouragement. Left to himself, he'd be running away. Can you think of a similar time in your life?

This wood is creepy-looking alright. There are crows and owls with eyes that glow eerily. The sign said it was haunted. The Scarecrow suggests, *"I believe there're spooks around here."* Did he know that the word "spook" comes from the Swedish word for "scarecrow"? Apparently not. He told us earlier that he wasn't afraid of anything except a lighted match. We wouldn't expect a scarecrow to be afraid of scarecrows.

Tin Man tries to be bold: *"That's ridiculous! Spooks! That's silly!"*

"D-don't you believe in spooks?" Lion stammers.

"No! Why, on — Oh!" Suddenly Tin Man vanishes straight up and is thrown to the ground with a loud crash a few feet up the path. Dorothy and Scarecrow rush to his aid. Thank God, he's well-built, even if he doesn't think so. He's resilient. He literally bounces back. That word, "resilient" is related to the first audible heartbeat of an embryo, which seems to leap into life, a new starting point. The Tin Man's heart is growing right in front of us. Knowing that we're well-made, that we're resilient, makes it possible for us to bounce back when we get knocked down.

Meanwhile, The Lion trembles with his eyes closed. This is probably something he's done many times before when cowardice has gotten the best of him. Twisting his tail, he mutters anxiously, *"I do believe in spooks, I do believe in spooks; I do, I do, I do, I do, I do."* His words have the form of a creed, a belief not in a caring God or of a loving companion, but of a sinister, unseen force. She hears his profession of faith. The scene shifts to the nearby dark fortress where The Witch sees The Lion in her crystal ball and cackles,

"You'll believe in more than that before I've finished with you!"

She commands an army of winged monkeys. In Frank Baum's book, the reader knows they're under a spell and must obey The Witch's orders. In the movie, we only see them as eager to do her evil bidding. *"Take your army to the Haunted Forest and bring me that girl and her dog. Do what you like with the others, but I want her alive and unharmed!"*

Her next line betrays a clumsy edit of the film, *"They'll give you no trouble. I promise you that. I've sent a little insect on ahead to take the bite out of them!"* It's a reference to what Ozophiles know as "the Jitterbug scene." In it Judy Garland sings of a bug with, *"a terrible, horrible buzz."* Its sting causes the characters to spin into an exhausting dancing frenzy. Only a fragment of the deleted scene still exists on film. It reminds me of how the Christian gospels were also the creative work of teams of storytellers and editors. In the Gospel of John at the end of Chapter 14, Jesus concludes a speech, saying, "Come, then! Let's go." But then they don't go. Jesus keeps talking for three more chapters; then at the beginning of Chapter 18, we read, "After this discourse, Jesus went out...."

The Witch shrieks, *"Take care of those ruby slippers — I want those most of all! Now fly — fly! Fly! Fly! Fly!"* The sky turns dark with a squadron of flying monkeys in battle formation. They swoop down on the travelers. Tin Man swings his ax, to no avail. They grab Dorothy and carry her away. *"Toto! Toto! Help, Toto!"* she cries. But he's scooped up and carried away too.

The others regather. *"Help! Help! Help!"* Scarecow cries. He's been torn limb from limb. Lion and Tin Man put him back together. He's taken the roughest beating of them all. Gather means to bring together, to unite in fellowship. While they gather him, he gathers them. They have yet another new mission. Scarecrow directs them, *"Put me together! We've got to find Dorothy!"*

CHAPTER 24

Using Words

"Don't stand there talking!
Put me together!
We've got to find Dorothy!"

-SCARECROW

"Preach the gospel at all times
and when necessary use words."

-ST. FRANCIS OF ASSISI

When Scarecrow cries, *"We've got to find Dorothy,"*

he's saying at the same time, *"We've got to find* Doro-theos, *the gift of God."*

For 12 years I was the director of All Saints Catholic Newman Center, the Catholic campus ministry at Arizona State University. When it was time to leave there, the community gave me a going-away party. After dinner some of my students put on a skit — not surprisingly with a "Wizard of Oz" theme. One student wore my Dominican habit, the robe I wear when I preach. He played the role of me, preaching. In every other sentence he interrupted himself to teach the derivation of a word, until the whole thing was an incomprehensible mess. Everyone roared.

When I got my turn to thank them, I told them that for 12 wonderful years I'd had the honor of being their "director," which is related to the word "rectum" and that all good things must come to an end.

As I've been writing, I've wondered if I've annoyed you with all this etymology. If what I'm writing ever gets published, I have to assume that an editor will have cleaned up any mess I've made here. But I want you to know why I keep bringing up what words mean, or a deeper possible level of meaning inside them. I'm not trying to show off or to be a know-it-all. The reason is, I'm a preacher.

Thirty years ago I entered the Catholic religious order founded in 1206 by Saint Dominic. We're normally called "The Dominicans," but our official name is "The Order of Preachers." My full name is Father Nathan (which, by the way, means "gift") Castle, O.P. (for Order of Preachers). I'm not just a preacher on Sunday; the "Holy Preaching" is first a way of being, a consciousness of being loved as part of the One Love, and welcoming that Love into me, and then letting that Love move through me.

When I hear The Scarecrow say, *"We've got to find Dorothy!"* I hear him say, "We've got to find the gift of God!"

This might be the preachiest chapter of this book, which is why I want you to know how I think about preaching. When I hear the words "preach," "preacher" or "preaching" used by people in a secular context, it's often with an apology that sounds like this: "I don't mean to preach, but ...." In the popular imagination, preachers, I think, speak from a power disequilibrium. Preachers stand on heights, above their hearers. They often have microphones, titles and the regalia of authority. But to preach means to announce, to proclaim, or simply, to say.

I started college as an art major. Paints, markers and watercolors were my media. I drew and painted until I knew that wasn't my calling. What did I end up being? A preacher, who uses words as his media. I try to paint in speech, or now, in writing, with words. I even have the audacity to take the beloved words of Frank Baum, a great word artist, and expand upon them.

I want to share with you how I understand what's most important to me: love, life and its meaning, and the love of God, who I believe is with all of us always. My goal isn't to persuade, convince and certainly not to prove. Do you remember, in the forest along the Yellow Brick Road, when the others were just coming to know The Lion? They helped him open his heart and they invited him along on their journey. Before breaking into his song, "If I Only Had the Nerve," he said, *"It's been in me so long I just gotta tell you how I feel."*

Once upon a time, 5,000 or a gazillion years ago, God spoke a creative word recorded in the Book of Genesis, "'Let there be light.' And there was light." (Genesis 1:3) And it came to pass that God said, "Let there be Nathan," and out of my parents' love I came to be. And God said, "Let there be you," and there was you. I believe that God, who loved me into being, lives in me and all around me. I believe that God lives in and around you too. And, yes, I believe God lives over the rainbow and beyond the farthest star. John's gospel begins with, "In the beginning was the Word; and the Word was in God's presence, and the Word was God. The Word became flesh and made his dwelling in us, and we have seen God's glory." (John 1:1,14) I believe God became enfleshed, became human, in the person of Jesus. He is simply love, as all of us are when we are stripped of every title and role. We're each a beautiful gift of God, enfleshed.

Many chapters ago I introduced the idea that, in the *Wizard of Oz* story, I see Toto as godly, like Jesus. Toto is love enfleshed. He is at home everywhere. He'll be with you whether you're at home, running away or trying to find your way when nothing looks familiar.

As the flying monkeys carry Dorothy away she cries from her heart, *"Toto! Toto! Help, Toto!"* What could her little dog possibly do to help? Well, he could be with her. He could go with her into the heart of darkness. How about you? Has love ever become enfleshed for you by the gift of the presence of someone who was with you in a dark time and place?

The screenplay reads, "Dorothy screams as she is carried over the trees. Another monkey grabs Toto and disappears." For now the community is dismembered. Dorothy is lost to them. The others are left picking up the pieces. How will they find Dorothy? They don't know it at the time, but very soon a little one will guide them. And he's been with them all along. He's really with them as he's carried away. He's still in their midst, between Dorothy and the others. Though temporarily separated against their will, Scarecrow, Tin Man and Lion are still united with Dorothy. And with Toto, too.

CHAPTER 25

Nobody's Home

The flying monkeys looked terrifying alright.

They have dragonlike wings. They swoop and grab their prey like raptors. Dorothy and Toto might have been eaten alive. Instead, in the next scene, we find them sound, if not safe. Toto is in The Witch's grasp.

"What a nice little dog," she coos with what the screenplay calls "diabolical sweetness." She puts him in a basket and closes the lid. *"And you, my dear, what an unexpected pleasure. It's so kind of you to visit me in my loneliness."*

We're in The Witch's home — and home is a major theme in *The Wizard of Oz* — but she's really not at home here or anywhere else. This castle was built to keep people out. It has, sadly, done its job too well. When she mentions, sarcastically, her loneliness, The Witch points to a painful truth about herself. What she doesn't do is what the other major characters are all doing, reimagining their lives and seeking positive change. She just wants more of the same. More domination, which will only bring a deeper loneliness.

One's *domus*, or domicile, can be a place of welcome to be freely shared. A generous-hearted person might say, *"Mi casa es su casa,"* "My house is your house." Loving always involves sharing oneself, inviting others in. Some castles are inhabited by a *dominus*, a lord who provides a safe place, a place of belonging for all in his domain. The Psalmist put it like this:

The Lord's are the earth and its fullness,

the world and all who dwell in it.

Psalm 24:1

It's possible to at least dream of a world where everyone is at home.

Or not. Anyone who wants to may choose to try to dominate others. Those who "lord it over" others, who succeed at domination, eventually find themselves home alone. The Witch's castle is populated with all those she dominates, the flying monkeys and the Winkie Guards, and for the moment, Dorothy and Toto. But it's nobody's home.

Dorothy is separated from Scarecrow, Tin Man and Lion for the first time since they became friends. Only Toto is with her — and maybe not for long.

"What are you going to do with my dog? Give him back to me," Dorothy demands.

"All in good time," The Witch replies snidely, *"all in good time."*

Dorothy goes from demanding to begging, *"Oh, please, give me back my dog!"*

"Certainly — certainly. When you give me those slippers." The Witch craves them for their powers, which she would use to dominate others. This has produced her isolation, and yet she wants more of it. Have you ever craved more of what is bad for you, even if possessing it would harm those around you?

Dorothy, a good girl at heart, can't comply. *"The Good Witch of the North told me not to."*

"Very well!" She barks a savage order to the monkey captain: *"Throw him into the river and drown him!"*

"No! No — no! Here, you can have your old slippers, but give me back Toto!"

The Witch grabs for them, and sparks fly! She shrieks in pain. Dorothy doesn't know what to say. First, she takes responsibility, and then she doesn't. *"I'm sorry. I didn't do it."* But can she still have her dog, she asks? Fat chance.

"No! Fool that I am! I should have remembered! Those slippers will never come off ... as long as you're alive."

This is taking an ugly turn.

"But that's not what's worrying me ... it's how to do it ... these things must be done delicately, or you'll hurt the spell ...."

And as The Witch ponders a gentle little murder, the triumph of death over life ...

Toto bolts.

He pushes the lid off the basket-that-would-be-casket ... and scrambles out the door. *"Run, Toto, Run,"* Dorothy cries. Her words are pure selfless love. She's still endangered, but the one she loves is free. Now she's more alone than ever, and overjoyed. At the window she sees Toto leap from the drawbridge landing safely on the other side. The guards' spears fall harmlessly around him. *"He got away. He got away!"* Dorothy shouts for joy. She has no way of knowing whether she'll ever see him again. Has Toto abandoned her in her hour of need? She doesn't see it that way. Toto has escaped death and she loves Toto. Under the shadow of her own death she rejoices. Toto got away! Have you ever known such a moment?

This is an important moment in my interpretation of the story and of Toto as a Christ figure who is "I AM with you always." For this is the only moment in the movie when Toto is *not* with Dorothy. Have you felt the apparent absence of God? What's Toto doing? What's God up to?

The Witch is angrier than ever. *"Drat you and your dog! You've been more trouble to me than you're worth one way and another, but it'll soon be over now!"* She seizes a large hourglass with its blood-red sand and flips it over. *"You see that? That's how much longer you have to be alive. And it isn't long my pretty, it isn't long!"* The Witch leaves the room, slamming the door and locking it.

Now Dorothy's home alone, in nobody's home.

CHAPTER 26

On a Mission

"*Bring me her broomstick and I'll grant your requests! Now go!*"

The Wizard commands, his anger simmering. When The Lion objects, *"But — but what if she kills us first?"* Oz's wrath blazes and expels them from his presence. *"I said GO!"*

They have their orders. They've been sent on a mission. There's a religious word for that — "apostle," the Greek word for one who has been sent on a mission.

The scene shifts to a haunted forest. A sign says "Witches Castle, 1 mile." Beneath it another sign reads, "I'd turn back if I were you." The Lion begins to oblige when The Tin Man and Scarecrow, without a word, "link their arms firmly in his and turn him back to face the right way." That's the advantage of an apostolic community over a solo mission; when one member falters, others can supply for their need.

The mission seemed impossibly large to all of them, especially to The Cowardly Lion. So why did they accept it? Two reasons are clear to the travelers.

Each one is pursuing his or her heart's desire, desires that have grown even stronger through trial. And they love each other. The more they share their lives, especially their challenges, the more their love grows.

One more reason is clearer to The Witch and to the viewer than to the characters on the journey. They keep getting unexpected help — right when they need it most. Back at the poppy field The Witch said it well, *"Curseit! Curseit!*

Somebody always helps that girl!" How many times does that have to happen before you begin to rely on the idea that you'll have what you need at the moment you most need it?

This is right up my alley. This is what I do for a living. I try to help form communities of people to embrace a common mission — not from fear, but from love. And that mission: to seek his or her own heart's desire while helping everyone else seek theirs. And to know that they'll always have Helpers, seen and unseen.

So what do you pack for this journey?

Jesus, leader of the upside-down, inside-out, last-shall-be-first, universal kingdom, gives this instruction for the mission: a list of what not to bring. "Take nothing for the journey. Don't take a walking staff. Don't take baggage. Don't bring food. Or money. Or extra clothes. Stay where you're welcomed and offer a blessing. If your blessing is received, great. If not, it will return to you. Don't let momentary defeat cling to you. Shake its dust from you and go on to the next place. Accept the gifts which you will be given. You'll do great things." (Luke 9 and 10)

Did you know that the film had three different directors? Different screenwriting teams came and went, too. They were filming without a finished script. For all of MGM's organization and movie-making know-how, this huge, expensive project was a seat-of-the-pants mission. This section of the film is the clumsiest.

Take a look at the travelers in the haunted forest scene; maybe even pause the film. The Scarecrow, who has been empty-handed until now, is carrying — I love this — a walking staff! And a water pistol. The Tin Man has his ax — but has added a massive pipe wrench, because … they might encounter plumbing problems? The Lion has an enormous butterfly net and a pump-spray can of "Witch Remover." In a bit of dialogue deleted from the movie, The Tin Man warns Dorothy she should have something to protect herself with. The Lion offers her the Witch Remover.

"Does it work?" she asks, doubtfully.

"No, but it's wonderful for threatening with," he admits, crestfallen.

All this unnecessary stuff disappears by virtue of editing. It literally landed on the cutting room floor. In the following scenes the travelers are carrying nothing but Dorothy's basket and Tin Man's ax, which they've had all along.

Now I think they're ready for the mission.

So Dorothy's all alone.

The travelers are without all the random stuff they started to bring along. Dorothy's been told she has only an hour to be alive, and she can watch it slip away like sand in the hourglass.

Now it's time for the gifts to emerge.

First, there's Toto, calling them to action. He scampers into a clearing where Tin Man and Lion are restuffing Scarecrow.

"Look! There's Toto! Where'd he come from?" Tin Man asks.

If you have The Scarecrow's gift of understanding, it's obvious. *"Why don't you see? He's come to take us to Dorothy!"*

Before you know it, they're scaling boulders with The Lion in the lead. He's not using his tail as a hanky anymore. Now it's a lifeline, enabling Tin Man to make the climb. They arrive at the crest of a ridge, the dark towers of the castle in view.

"What's that? What's that?" Lion asks.

Scarecrow, the answerman, replies, *"That's the castle of the Wicked Witch! Dorothy's in that awful place?"*

Tin Man's heart is breaking. *"Oh, I hate to think of her in there. We've got to get her out."* And he's got to get that heart of his pumping. When we first met him he was singing,

"I'd be tender, I'd be gentle
and awful sentimental
regarding love and art..."

But today's not Valentine's Day. The Scarecrow rebukes him bluntly, *"Don't cry now. We haven't got the oil can with us, and you've been creaking enough as it is!"* But remember, there was more to Tin Man's song:

"When a man's an empty kettle
he should be on his mettle
and yet I'm torn apart..."

Well, The Scarecrow has become something of an expert on being torn apart. He knows the mission calls for everyone's gifts — and they need the metal man's mettle. They need him to show what he's made of. And there's no time to waste.

190

Suddenly, "a dozen enormous Winkie guards holding wicked-looking weapons appear below them" marching and chanting. What they need now is a military strategist. One emerges:

"I've got a plan how to get in there," Scarecrow announces, *"… and you're going to lead us,"* he commands The Lion.

Lion's cowardice and courage fight for control. *"I've gotta get her outta there? All right, I'll go in there for Dorothy — Wicked Witch or no Wicked Witch — guards or no guards — I'll tear 'em apart — Woof! I may not come out alive, but I'm goin' in there! There's only one thing I want you fellas to do."*

"What's that?" they ask.

"Talk me out of it!"

Instead they prevent his retreat and push him to the front.

But three huge Winkie guards rise above them from behind and pounce. We hear The Lion shout, *"Put 'em up!"* He's not picking on the weak anymore. When the fight comes to them, they hold their ground. We can't see its progress.

Soon "the sounds of the fray die down." Have Dorothy's friends been killed?

Three Winkie helmets peek above the rocks. Tin Man, Scarecrow and Lion appear dressed in the heavy Winkie uniforms. Even Toto has a tassel in his mouth.

Scarecrow had a plan, but the plans have changed. *"Come on, I've got another idea."*

The three slip into the marching Winkie procession. With Toto bringing up the rear, they enter The Witch's castle. Those uniforms really did the trick. They hadn't packed extra clothes, remember? But these were delivered to them at just the right time.

Once inside, things happen fast.

"*Where do we go now?*" Tin Man asks.

But Toto's already on the job. He barks from the stairs and leads them to an upper room. He barks and scratches at the door.

"*Wait! We'd better make sure. Dorothy? Are you in there?*" Scarecrow shouts.

"*Yes, it's me! She's locked me in!*"

They shed their uniforms and drop their spears.

"*Stand back!*" Tin Man shouts. He has what is needed. He begins to smash the door with his ax. The splintered door flies open.

Dorothy falls into their arms, as Scarecrow hands her Toto. "*Oh-oh-oh, Toto! Toto!*" To all of them she says, "*I knew you'd come! I knew you would!*"

"*Hurry — we've got no time to lose!*" Scarecrow leads them away. Just as they reach the open entrance doors, they slam shut. A burst of savage laughter fills the room.

The Witch cackles: "*Going so soon? I wouldn't hear of it! Why, my little party's just beginning!*" From above she hurls the hourglass to the floor below. It explodes like a bomb. The room fills with Winkie guards, their spears thrust at the travelers.

"*That's right. Don't hurt them right away. We'll let them think about it a little first,*" The Witch laughs.

Bad idea, lady. You're about to be out-thunk.

Scarecrow spies the heavy chandelier above the Winkies. He sees it's suspended by a rope tied to a hook next to them on the wall. He jerks The Tin Man's arm so his ax severs the rope. The huge candelabra falls on the Winkies.

Scarecrow grabs Dorothy, who's holding Toto. Tin Man and Lion are close behind. They dash through the Winkie lines and rush into a courtyard.

There's lots of running this way and that. The Witch's castle is a dark maze. They retreat to a dark tower, where they're surrounded again. This looks like the end.

The Witch laughs, *"Well! Ring-around-the rosy! A pocketful of spears! Thought you'd be pretty foxy, didn't cha? Well, the last to go will see the first three go before her … and her mangy little dog, too!"*

The Witch touches her broom to a burning torch on the wall. *"How about a little fire, Scarecrow?"*

He jumps up and down — his arm is on fire! *"Oh! No! No! No! Help! I'm burning! I'm burning! Help!"*

Dorothy suddenly sees a bucket of water. She puts Toto down and hurls the bucket.

Before The Witch can finish saying, *"Don't touch that water!"* the flames are extinguished and The Witch is soaking wet. She screams and writhes in agony. She's melting.

"Ohhh! You cursed brat! Look what you've done! I'm melting! Melting! Oh, what a world! What a world! Who would have thought

a good little girl like you could destroy my beautiful wickedness! Ohhh! Look out! Look out! I'm going! Ohhhh — Ohhhhhhhhhh!"

Who knew it could be so simple? All they needed, in the end, was water. It washes away evil. It cleanses, refreshes and marks a new beginning. A new cycle of life begins.

And a new mission. They have the broomstick. Now they can go back to The Wizard, redeem it and claim their hearts' desires.

CHAPTER 27

Not So Fast

When the travelers return

to Emerald City with the broomstick, they expect prompt service. They make their way up the aisle of The Wizard's sham church. Dorothy steps up to the counter at the transactional religion store. She addresses the clerk: *"…We've done what you told us: We've brought you the broomstick of The Wicked Witch of the West … so we'd like you to keep your promise to us, if you please, sir."*

Oz, the surly disincarnate head on the wall, won't be rushed. He barks, *"Not so fast! Not so fast!"*

The action has moved very rapidly of late. There was no time to waste. Several times in recent scenes someone wanted a moment to ponder something or to savor an emotion. Sometimes we need a little time just to reflect on our lives and to be grateful before we ask for more, however entitled we might believe ourselves to be.

When you slow down, try on some of these questions:

Has your life had its missions?

Were there times when you were sent to accomplish an important task?

Who were your companions?

What gifts did they have or lack?

Have you had to rely on others who weren't always sure of themselves?

Have you had to go up against long odds feeling that you lacked something essential?

Did you ever pack too much stuff, only to find that life works better when you travel light?

Have you been surprised by grace … those timely unexpected gifts that change everything?

Have you had to move through disappointment and defeat, only to move on to the next chapter of your life?

I'd like to take us back to the scene in the gospel story where Jesus sent out inexperienced but eager apostles and invited them to change the world.

Things must have gone very well for them. The text is short on detail, but they came back "in jubilation, saying, 'Master, even the demons are subject to us in your name.'" Jesus replies, "I saw Satan fall from the sky like lightning… Nevertheless, do not rejoice so much in the fact that devils are subject to you as that your names are inscribed in heaven." (Luke 10:17)

"She's — she's dead. You've killed her," the leader of the Winkies says, his former master reduced to a steaming puddle on the floor.

"I didn't mean to kill her — really I didn't — it's just that he was on fire." Even in the heat of the moment, Dorothy has to reflect on her experience and check her motives.

But the Winkies drop to their knees. Dorothy scores the genuflection The Lion thought he'd deserve if he were King of the Forest.

Dorothy keeps her head. She isn't rejoicing in her power over anyone. *"The broom! May we have it?"* Remember, getting that broom was the point of the mission. Or at least of the submission. This was just one part of a much larger story arc. Her friends' and her hearts' desires will only be theirs when she brings The Wizard this now-scorched janitorial item.

"Hail to Dorothy! The Wicked Witch is dead!" the Winkies shout from their knees. The last time she inadvertently killed a wicked witch the Munchkins promised she'd, *"be a bust, be a bust, be a bust, be a bust in the Hall of Fame!"*

Is Dorothy wise beyond her years, or simply good? While Oz's ego expands out of control, monstrously magnified on the wall of his inner sanctum, Dorothy wants only to help her friends and then do the one thing she's been trying to do, the one thing this whole journey's been about all along. She wants to go home. She's already had her name written in the sky, remember? She knows there's a place where her name is written on others' hearts. She wants to be there.

She will be soon enough. Just not so fast as she thought.

CHAPTER 28

Confirmation

Dorothy and Toto, Scarecrow, Tin Man and Lion

now stand where they've stood before. Nothing has changed. But everything's different.

The Wizard of Oz played upon their fears before, and he tries to again. Shouting has always seemed to work.

"Can I believe my eyes? Why have you come back?" Oz bellows.

Dorothy explains, *"Please, sir, we've done what you told us: We've brought you the broomstick of The Wicked Witch of the West. We melted her."*

But there's no pleasing him. *"Go away and come back tomorrow!"* Oz booms, with more flames, more smoke.

They stand their ground. They've been in scarier places than this. Dorothy speaks, *"Tomorrow? Oh, but I want to go home now!"*

Tin Man's been in the background most of the time, except when his ax was needed. Now he finds his voice: *"You've had plenty of time already!"*

The not-so-Cowardly Lion agrees. He growls, *"Yeah!"*

So Oz roars still louder, *"Do not arouse the wrath of the Great and Powerful Oz! I said come back tomorrow!"* Poor Oz is a one-trick pony. If he can't strike the fear of God into you, the show's over.

"If you were really great and powerful, you'd keep your promises!" Dorothy scolds.

"Do you presume to criticize the Great Oz?" His act is dying.

And then Toto pulls aside the curtain.

When Jesus dies, the text reads like this: "Once again Jesus cried out in a loud voice, and released his spirit. Suddenly the curtain of the sanctuary was torn in two from top to bottom." (Matthew 27:50-51)

No more separation, or distance, or falsehood. The Spirit of "I AM with you" is also the Spirit of truth and peace.

Suddenly unmasked, Oz pulls the curtain back again, but it's curtains for this tired act. *"Pay no attention to that man behind the curtain! The Great Oz has spoken!"*

Dorothy, gift of God, walks up quietly and pulls the curtain aside. *"Who are you?"* she asks.

His reply is half-amplified, half-muttered: *"I AM THE GREAT AND POWERFUL … Wizard of Oz."*

"I don't believe you."

"No, I'm afraid it's true. There's no other Wizard except me."

Upon arriving in Munchkinland, the first words spoken to Dorothy were, *"Are you a good witch or a bad witch?"* She's grown up in a black-and-white world of polar opposites. She makes a rash judgment. *"Oh, you're a very bad man."*

"Oh, no, my dear, I — I'm a very good man — I'm just a very bad wizard."

The temptation toward wizardry is everywhere you look. So many people have not been loved for who they are, and have instead settled for being praised for what they do, assuming they do something well. It's never enough. There's a "soul hunger" no amount of applause can satisfy. This unmasked man talking to Dorothy, whoever he is, hasn't wasted his whole life. At some quiet moment in his lonely palace he was given the gift of knowledge. He knows he's a very good man — who's just a very bad wizard.

Scarecrow angrily refocuses the conversation, *"What about the heart you promised Tin Man? And the courage that you promised Cowardly Lion?"*

Tin Man and Lion quickly add: *"And Scarecrow's brain?"*

The Wizard, for all his faults, has been around. He knows something about people. He knows they sometimes need help seeing in themselves qualities that are easily recognized by those around them.

I remember how weird I got in the last few weeks before I became a priest. I'd been in training for it for seven years, but as ordination day approached I wondered if I was really ready for it. After your first Mass people wait in line to kneel before you and ask a blessing. People twice and three times your age come to you for advice. They tell you their secrets and invite you behind their curtain. It all just seemed too large, and I felt too small. I was asking priests I'd known for years, "What will it be like to be a priest?"

The answer I got didn't come from any one individual. It came from the community as a whole. It sounded like this:

Don't worry. It's not magic. You've been becoming a priest, growing into the gift of your priesthood all your life, especially in recent years.

We've tried to help you and have watched you grow. We think you're ready and we need what God will give us through you.

There's a moment in the ordination ceremony when a senior priest, on behalf of a team of formators, is asked, "Is he ready?" With a word he tells the community:

"It's time." The people confirm that reply with their applause. The bishop then prays the laying on of hands, anoints the hands of the ordinand and someone, in my case my parents, comes forward and dresses the new priest in stole and chasuble.

Did I become a priest on my ordination day? Sure. But I was becoming one long before that day arrived. With a lot of help from a lot of people.

I've mentioned earlier that this Professor Marvel/Wizard of Oz character has dabbled in a sham shamanism. But now he's in the heart of his priesthood. These people before him are asking to have gifts conferred. He knows he hasn't the power to confer their gifts, but he can confirm them. They just need a sacramental — an outward, visible sign, a token, of the inner, invisible reality.

Up first is Scarecrow.

"Why, anybody can have a brain. That's a very mediocre commodity. Every pusillanimous creature that crawls on the earth or slinks through slimy seas has a brain! Back where I come from, we have universities, seats of great learning — where men go to become great thinkers, and when they come out, they think deep thoughts — and with no more brains than you have — but! They have one thing you haven't got! A diploma. Therefore — by virtue of the authority vested in me by the Universitatus Committeeatum e pluribus unum, I hereby confer upon you the honorary degree of Th.D!"

"Th.D.?" Scarecrow asks.

"Yeah, that ... that's Doctor of Thinkology."

Scarecrow immediately blurts out, *"The sum of the square roots of any two sides of an isosceles triangle is equal to the square root of the remaining side. Oh joy, rapture! I've got a brain!"*

Never mind that that's not exactly right. What he says is true of equilateral triangles, but why rain on his parade? He's got a brain!

Next, it's The Lion.

"As for you, my fine friend, you're a victim of disorganized thinking. You are under the unfortunate delusion that simply because you run away from danger, you have no courage. You're confusing courage with wisdom."

Courage is that gift which makes all the other gifts more durable under fire. Lion has proven he has it.

"Back where I come from, we have men who are called heroes. Once a year they take their fortitude out of mothballs and parade it down the main street of the city. And they have no more courage than you have — but! They have one thing that you haven't got! A medal! Therefore, for meritorious conduct, extraordinary valor, conspicuous bravery against wicked witches, I award you the Triple Cross. You are now a member of the Legion of Courage."

Oz pins on the medal and kisses Lion on both cheeks. Lion tells us, *"Shucks, folks, I'm speechless!"* He's humble, too.

Now it's Tin Man's turn.

"As for you, my galvanized friend, you want a heart! You don't know how lucky you are not to have one. Hearts will never be practical until they can be made unbreakable."

"But I ... I still want one," Tin Man adds.

"Back where I come from, there are men who do nothing all day but good deeds. They are called phil ... er ... phil ... er ... yes ... er ... good-deed-doers, and their hearts are no bigger than yours — but — they have one thing you haven't got! A testimonial!

Therefore, in consideration of your kindness, I take pleasure at this time in presenting you with a small token of our esteem and affection."

He hands Tin Man a huge heart-shaped watch and chain.

"And remember, my sentimental friend, that a heart is not judged by how much you love, but how much you are loved by others."

I wonder about that. Some very loving people find their love unreturned. Jesus, for example, comes to mind. At the moment he was loving them most, his closest friends ran away. I've known plenty of underloved lovers, haven't you? Really heroic love can cause all sorts of trouble.

But sometimes we do see brilliant examples of how much people are loved by others. At graduations and anniversaries, going-away parties and retirement celebrations … and especially around funerals you can often see how very much a person is loved by others.

Judging others' hearts isn't our job anyway. That's best left to God. I prefer the way the beloved Prayer of St. Francis puts it:

Oh, Master, grant that I may never seek,

So much to be consoled as to console,

To be understood as to understand,

To be loved as to love with all my soul.

CHAPTER 29

Into Thin Air

"Oh, I'd give anything to get out of Oz

altogether; but which is the way to Kansas? I can't go the way I came!"

That logic seemed so clear back when Dorothy stood in the spiral that marked the beginning of the Yellow Brick Road. You can't board the next cyclone to Kansas like you board a boat or a train. We sometimes speak of hard-won progress as "two steps forward and one step back." In Dorothy's case it might be 2,000 steps forward and one step back. But it's a very big one step back.

She had just seen her friends' dreams come true. Their gifts grew from within, step by step, until they were magnificently intelligent, loving and courageous. But when it came her turn she said sadly, *"Oh I don't think there's anything in that black bag for me."*

She lost hope.

She's done this before, most notably when she gave up on earth and traded it in for somewhere, anywhere over the rainbow. Toto and she had unmasked the man behind the curtain — but only for a moment — before she was again inviting him back into wizardry. One minute the wind's blowing one way, then another. We're spinning again. It's thrilling, even dizzying in that moment right before the storm.

I remember as a child how the air felt different before an approaching storm.

You could see the treetops swirling and dark clouds massing. There was an exhilarating smell and something electric in the air. Sometimes you could see a downpour in the next block before feeling a single raindrop. The humbug wizard proclaims to Dorothy, *"Well, you force me in to a cataclysmic decision."* "Cataclysm" means a downpour or deluge. My sister, Cathryn, remembers how, before an approaching storm, we'd "do twirlybirds" on the front lawn, spinning around like crazy people.

That's what Emerald City's square looks like to me — a crowd whipped into a frenzy. This is what The Wizard does best; he can really work a crowd.

There's a decorated platform in the center of the square. The Wizard's balloon is moored to it. In its basket are The Wizard, Dorothy and Toto.

"My friends," The Wizard shouts, *"This is possibly the finest exhibition ever to be shown … well … eh … well … be that as it may — I, your Wizard … am about to embark upon a hazardous and technically unexplainable journey into the outer stratosphere."*

The crowd goes wild.

"… to confer, converse, and otherwise hobnob with my brother wizards."

Apparently, the truth that he's giving the girl and her dog a ride home lacks pizzaz. He spins the story. He mentions the trip will involve "hazards." That word derives from a bad roll of dice. This balloon ride is a crapshoot. He'll "hobnob" with other wizards, he says. To hobnob means to buy alternate rounds of drinks in a crowd. The atmosphere is intoxicating. With one sentence he leaves Scarecrow, Tin Man and Lion in charge. He ends his speech with a grand, *"Thank you!"* And they're off.

When suddenly, Toto, the canine face of God, spies a cat. Barking, he leaps from the balloon basket. *"Oh, Toto! Come back! Toto! Toto!"* Dorothy cries, jumping out and chasing after him.

The scene gets crazier. Scarecrow and Lion drop the mooring ropes to help Dorothy. The balloon begins to rise.

"This is a highly irregular procedure! … absolutely unprecedented!" The Wizard cries, trying to save the scene.

"Oh, help me!" Tin Man cries. *"The balloon's going up!"*

As he leaves the ground The Wizard thinks nothing of Dorothy's dashed hopes. *"Ruined my exit!"* he says, a showman to the end.

As he rises, Dorothy screams, *"Oh, come back, come back — don't leave without me! Please come back!"*

"I can't come back! I don't know how it works!" The Wizard waves to the cheering crowd. *"Good-bye, folks!"* he cries as he drifts out of sight.

The Wizard is a drunk driver. There's probably another ditch in his future.

But Dorothy has missed her ride. Her hope vanishes into thin air. In terrible distress she cries, *"Oh, now I'll never get home."* But home is closer than she's dared hope.

CHAPTER 30

Sterile

It looks like the end of the line for Dorothy, and she says so. *"Now I'll never get home."*

But home is where the heart is. Dorothy and Toto have entered the hearts of Lion, Scarecrow and the officially large-hearted Tin Man. Lion offers an alternative, *"Stay with us then, Dorothy. We all love ya. We don't want you to go."*

She acknowledges the kindness of the offer, but this whole journey has been about her heart's desire. She might not know what her future is, but she knows what it isn't. *"This could never be like Kansas. Oh, Scarecrow, what am I going to do?"*

As I write, the school year is tilting toward graduation. This year's seniors are full of stories of the graduate programs they have or haven't gotten accepted into. Beloved projects and responsibilities are being handed over to the next set of leaders. Those in romantic relationships must decide what comes next: Do we stay together, date long-distance or separate?

I chose to leave all my friends behind after college and move many states and one huge state away. I felt called to try out a Catholic seminary. I was afraid I'd be really lonely. One day I was sitting beside a lake on the seminary property. At the base of the hill on which its buildings sat was a small town. That day a young woman from the town was out for a walk. She sat down next to me. "You must be a seminarian." "That's right," I said. She was quiet for a long time. Then she said, "Then that means you're sterile."

She meant celibate.

I'd decided to play it safe in this new place. Instead of opening myself to new people, I spent most of my free time writing long snail-mail letters to friends far away whom I missed so much. I knew I'd only be at this new place for a year in any event, so why bother to befriend another group of people I'd never see again?

Before long that year was over. That place helped me decide that I could commit to the journey toward serving God and God's people as a priest. I wanted to thank it and to say goodbye.

On my last day there my Volkswagen Rabbit was packed with everything I owned. There was just barely room for me. I got behind the wheel. Through the windshield was the wall of the chapel. I wanted to say goodbye and thank you and "have a good life" to someone. So I went back inside and began to walk the halls hoping to run into someone. I didn't. I hadn't befriended anyone. I realized that that girl was right: I was sterile.

So I got back into the Rabbit and said a prayer to the Friend of my Heart: "Hello in there. OK, I get it. No more looking back. No more guarding my heart. Come with me to the next place and help me love its people ... I'll do it even if it hurts."

"Now I know I have a heart ... 'cause it's breaking," cries The Tin Man, risking rusting.

By now Glinda the Good has floated in inside her bubble and has come to rest amid the travelers.

Dorothy grabs at another rescuer. *"Oh, will you help me? Can you help me?"*

"You don't need to be helped any longer. You've always had the power to go back to Kansas."

"I have?" Dorothy asks.

"Then why didn't you tell her before?" asks The Scarecrow on behalf of anyone with half a brain.

"Because she had to learn it herself," says Glinda, smiling.

Scarecrow and Tin Man offer Dorothy the only help she really needs. They ask the right question. *"What have you learned, Dorothy?"*

My dad could have written that line. That question was always part of his disciplining. *"What have you learned?"* I try to ask myself that one often.

"Well, I ... I think that it ... that it wasn't enough just to want to see Uncle Henry and Auntie Em." Reunions can be pleasant enough. But what makes for real growth in grace and wisdom? *"And it's that if I ever go looking for my heart's desire again, I won't look any further than my own backyard; because if it isn't there, I never really lost it to begin with!"*

Then she asks Glinda, *"Is that right?"*

"That's all it is."

"But that's so easy! I should have thought of it for you!" offers Scarecrow.

"I should have felt it in my heart!" adds Tin Man.

"No — she had to find it out for herself. Now those magic slippers will take you home in two seconds," Glinda says.

"Oh! Toto, too?"

"Toto, too."

"Now?" Dorothy asks, overjoyed.

"Whenever you wish."

"It's too wonderful to be true," Dorothy adds, but realizes right away, *"It's going to be hard to say goodbye. I love you all, too."*

The goodbyes that follow don't seem temporary. They seem more like the deathbed variety. There's a finality about them that seems profound and permanent. Dorothy whispers in Scarecrow's ear and gives him a teary kiss. *"I think I'll miss you most of all."*

"Are you ready now?" Glinda asks gently.

"Yes," Dorothy answers. *"Say goodbye Toto,"* waving his paw at them. *"I'm ready now."*

CHAPTER 31

No Place Like Home

"*Then close your eyes and tap your heels together three times....*"

The ruby slippers fill the screen. They click together three times.

"*...and think to yourself, 'There's no place like home; there's no place like home; there's no place like home.'*"

Dorothy repeats the phrase, mantra-like. It's a simple meditative practice anyone can do. It helps her move into her heart of hearts. Now she's really ready to encounter those who live there.

Do you wish you had magic shoes? Do you also wish you had a degree conferred by the Universitatus Committeeatum e pluribus unam, a heart-shaped clock, and a little tin badge? It's really not about the shoes, is it?

Dorothy, God's gift to the world, moves into her heart and commits to living there. No more chasing rainbows for her. She's reached the rainbow's end and has found her heart's desire.

How do you show this profound, transformative moment on a movie screen? The folks at MGM chose pulsing concentric circles superimposed over Dorothy, drawing the eye toward a diminishing point in the center. And, in Dorothy's case, her house spinning, spiraling, seen from below and homing in on earth.

There's a noise and a slight bump. It isn't scary. We're on the ground. We're back in Kansas.

Now we're looking down upon Dorothy, in black and white, safe in her bed. She's still repeating her mantra: *"There's no place like home; there's no place like home; there's no place like home."*

Auntie Em applies a damp cloth to her forehead. *"Wake up, honey,"* she says with a sweetness and softness we haven't really seen until now. *"Dorothy — Dorothy dear … it's Aunt Em, darling."*

"Oh, Auntie Em, it's you…."

"Yes, darling."

We hear Professor Marvel's voice before he appears at the window: *"Hello, there! Anybody home?"* That's a question it could take a lifetime to answer, to say yes to, isn't it? *"Anybody home?"* Dorothy's journey has taken her over the rainbow and back, but before she can answer, the professor says, *"I … I just dropped by because I heard the little girl got caught in the big …."*

He sees Dorothy and smiles.

"Well, she seems all right now."

"Yeah, she got quite a bump on the head. We kinda thought there for a minute she was going to leave us," Uncle Henry adds.

"But I did leave you, Uncle Henry," Dorothy replies earnestly, sitting up in the bed. *"That's just the trouble! And I tried to get back for days and days…."*

Aunt Em doesn't want her getting too excited: *"There, there, lie quiet now. You just had a bad dream."* Remember back in the barnyard, before the cyclone, Em had said, *"Now, Dorothy dear — stop imagining things … you always get yourself into a fret over nothing."*

"No…." Dorothy says. But before she can argue the point a crowd gathers. The three farmhands appear and reintroduce themselves in the order in which we met their alter egos along the Yellow Brick Road.

"Sure — remember me? Your old pal, Hunk?"

"Me, Hickory?"

"You couldn't forget my face, could you?"

No, she couldn't and neither can we. The faces of the people she loved and had just said a final goodbye to a moment ago are again right in front of her, just the same. Only different. Something has shifted.

"No, but it wasn't a dream," Dorothy begins, trying to make sense of a mystery too big for words. *"It was a place."* Pointing first to the three, she explains, *"And you — and you — and you,"* and, finally to the professor, *"and you were there!"*

They all laugh.

Dorothy is puzzled. *"But you couldn't have been, could you?"* It's hard to explain when worlds collide. *"Oh we dream lots of silly things when we…."* Auntie Em interjects dismissively, without finishing her sentence. When we what, Em? Get hit in the head with flying, tornadic debris?

Never mind.

Dorothy declares her own profession of faith. *"No, Aunt Em, this was a real truly live place. And I remember that some of it wasn't very nice — but most of it was beautiful! But just the same, all I kept saying to everybody was, 'I want to go home. And they sent me home!'"*

She waits for a reaction, but they all just laugh again.

"Doesn't anybody believe me?"

The screenplay says Uncle Henry's next line is delivered, "soberly, softly." I think it's delivered lamely, unconvincingly. *"Of course we believe you, Dorothy...."* Well, it's the thought that counts, isn't it?

And from off screen, from the foot of the bed Toto appears, making his way across the quilt, settling in Dorothy's arms, over her heart.

"Oh, but anyway, Toto, we're home — home! And this is my room — and you're all here — and I'm not going to leave here ever again, because I love you all! And ... oh, Auntie Em, there's no place like home!"

The music crescendos as it used to do in the golden age of the silver screen. The scene fades out. Two words fade in:

The End.

The End
And a New Beginning

So the movie ends but the story lives on.

Do you remember the dedication at the beginning of the film, made 40 years after the story was written?

> *"For nearly forty years this story has given faithful service to the*
> *Young in Heart; and Time has been powerless to put its kindly*
> *philosophy out of fashion. To those of you who have been*
> *faithful to it in return … and to the Young in Heart —*
> *we dedicate this picture."*

Now the movie is 72 years old; the book is a spry 111. My little book adds a bit more to the ongoing life of "The Wizard of Oz."

The original book was so popular that Frank Baum had to keep writing more stories about these characters. I haven't read them. I'd rather use my own imagination. I think that's part of having the heart of a child.

So when Dorothy says, *"I'm not going to leave here ever, ever again,"* what do you think happens next? Does she live the rest of her life in that farmhouse? Who knows? Maybe she does, but it won't be because of fear. She's forever changed by all that's happened in Oz. I think she'll fly away again — when it's time to — and fly back from time to time to visit those she loves. Or maybe I just think that because that's what I've done. My family gave me wings. I'm still using them.

Dorothy, Em and Henry will have to deal with Almira Gulch. Maybe penitent Dorothy goes to bed without supper. Or Toto spends some time on a leash. Maybe Almira accepts an invitation to Sunday dinner at the Gale farm and after the meal they play checkers in the parlor.

The point is, movies end but lives don't. Not ever. Dorothy has had a foretaste of that. Those she'd said a tearful goodbye to were given back to her, only slightly different, in the next scene.

Many of the characters in *The Wizard of Oz* love each other, or grow to love each other. But in the screenplay, at least, you have to wait all the way to the next-to-last scene to hear anyone say so. The balloon has left without her and she's stuck forever in Oz when the teary-eyed King of the Forest, using the royal "we," speaks for everyone, *"Stay with us, then, Dorothy. We all love ya."* Moments later, delighted with the knowledge that she can go home in two seconds, Dorothy cries, *"…it's going to be so hard to say goodbye. I love you all, too."* And back in Kansas, where she can't make herself fully understood, she decides it doesn't matter. *"Oh, but anyway, Toto, we're home — home! … and I love you all. And … oh, Auntie Em, there's no place like home."*

The day I woke up Daddy was the first time I ever really said the words "I love you" and really heard them back. That wasn't "The End" of anything, just another day in our two lives. I mentioned back in the prologue that near the time of my father's death he said to me, "Whatever you did that day, do more of it. It really matters."

The truth is he told me that after he had made his journey and had arrived back home. The day after his funeral.

But that's another story.

Questions for Discussion

And Toto, Too

How do you feel about taking this kind of journey?

How do you answer the God question, or do you? Are you a believer in Something or Someone?

Would you identify yourself as agnostic, atheist or "none of the above"?

How comfortable do you feel about self-reflection?

Chapter 4 **The Characters**

In looking at your own life, what is it like to consider yourself as God's gift to the world?

"We're surrounded daily by familiar faces we barely know, some of them in our own households." What is your experience with this?

"Toto, I believe, is a Christ figure in *The Wizard of Oz*." What do you think about this?

Chapter 5 **Watching the Movie**

What do you think about infinity and your place in it?

Aunt Em and Uncle Henry are busy providing for Dorothy, while not providing for her. Have you ever found yourself in a similar scene?

How would you feel if you had the opportunity to start over in your relationships? Do you think that's possible in this world or the next?

Can you imagine a place where there isn't any trouble?

Would you go to such a place? Have you been to such a place?

CHAPTER 6 **Going No Place**

Think of a time when you felt like giving up.

Have you ever felt "they" were all against you? When? Why?

"God can be found in the oddest places in the oddest forms."

Can you think of instances in your own life where this has been true?

CHAPTER 7 **Marvelous Encounter**

How do you recognize a fellow traveler when you see one? What experiences in your life's journey have equipped you to help fellow travelers?

Professor Marvel helped Dorothy reimagine her circumstance. When has someone done that for you? What was that like?

When have you felt that you have been understood? On whose shoulders do you stand?

CHAPTER 8 **A Storm's Blowin' Up**

If you've ever been caught in your own private cyclone, what was it like?

"Love gives her the power to reverse her direction."

When have you experienced this kind of power?

What effect did it have?

What events ever caused you to "put down your baggage" and embrace what matters most?

Have you ever experienced a deep peace in the eye of the storm?

CHAPTER 9 **Over the Rainbow**

Have you ever gotten exactly what you wished for? What was it like?

What do you think of the idea of latent gifts lying dormant in you?

Have you experienced a gift emerging in you exactly when it was needed?

Glinda advises Dorothy to seek The Wizard's help in getting back home. Was this good advice or a bum steer? How do you feel when well-meaning folks offer you unsolicited advice?

CHAPTER 10 **Spiraling**

Have you ever had to live in ink, where no mistakes were tolerated?

Have you ever done a major "turning around?"

Do you think of your life as "something beautiful you're in the process of creating?"

CHAPTER 11 **Life's Way**

When you think of your life, do you consider it as a timeline or a circle?

"Death, like birth, is temporary. Both are followed by new life."

What do you think about that?

How do you respond to these questions:

"Can you ever finish loving those you love?" "Why would you want to?"

CHAPTER 12 **Do You Believe in Dog?**

"I will love you but I must be in control of our relationship at every moment."

If you experienced this in your life, how did it make you feel?

Can you imagine God choosing to be weak in order to love?

"Believer" and "Beloved" are from the same root.

What do you believe about love from someone who considers you beloved?

CHAPTER 13 **At a Crossroads**

Think of a time when you followed your joy. Were you glad you did?

When have you done work for which you were very ill-suited?

"Where did Dorothy's earlier apprehension go? It melted away in the presence of a new companion on the journey." When has something like this happened to you?

CHAPTER 14 **Echoes of Eden**

The apple tree didn't want to feed Dorothy but it is very willing to hurl its fruit at her like missiles. When have you behaved like that?

Can you think of a time when a healing word changed you?

When have you offered a healing word?

Tin Man blames his creator for his lack of a heart.

What have you blamed your creator for?

When have you ever been made to feel subhuman?

Did anyone ever love you at a time you felt unlovable?

CHAPTER 15 **Fear and Courage**

Have you ever talked yourself into being afraid?

Or joined your voice to a chorus of doomsayers?

Have you ever been bullied? Or been a bully? What did the experience teach you?

What has made you most fearful? What has made you most courageous?

CHAPTER 16 **Playing Witch's Advocate**

Is there anyone you'd like to hate that you haven't properly met?

Do you believe it's true that everyone has some good in them?

Have you ever loved an enemy?

CHAPTER 17 **Sleeping And Waking, Dying And Rising**

Do you believe you will survive your death?

"Lots of people want to believe in a listening God who hears their prayers, but are unsure that their prayers matter at all, especially in life-and-death situations."

What do you think?

The Scarecrow cries "Help!" and is heard and helped.

When has this happened to you?

How do you feel about the hope of being reunited with loved ones upon your death?

CHAPTER 18 **The Title Character**

Have you ever acted within a role that became your identity?

Do you think there's a little of The Wizard in all of us?

Have you ever had to admit that you're a very good person, but a very bad wizard?

Chapter 19 **Pilgrims**

If you went on a pilgrimage where would you go? What would you seek?

Whom in your life do you feel bound together with on a common journey?

Chapter 20 **If I Were King**

Was there ever a time when you longed to be respected — to be given a second look? Did it happen?

Was there ever a time when you craved a leadership position for the status it would give you? Did you grow into something deeper?

Think of a time when someone encouraged you before you had your own courage. What was that like?

Chapter 21 **Caution**

When have you had to override a cautiousness you were taught?

Think of a time when you had to find the courage to initiate a difficult conversation. How did it go?

Have you ever been relieved to hear a difficult truth?

Is there anyone, living or deceased, you'd like to have an important conversation with?

Chapter 22 **Unholy Encounter**

What experience have you had of being turned away rudely by someone who was supposed to represent the holy?

Were you ever moved to compassionate action unexpectedly?

In what scary places has your life landed you?

CHAPTER 23 **Regathering**

Do you think it's possible for humans not to hate? For you not to hate?

Can you look back upon a time when life got hardest right when
you had nothing left to give? What did you do?

What do you do when you need to regather?

CHAPTER 24 **Using Words**

Recall a time when someone was present with you in a dark time or place.

Would you consider that a time of love becoming enfleshed for you?

Do you believe your being is a gift to the world?

Were you ever in a circumstance in which you wanted to do something to help
but your presence was all you really had to offer?

CHAPTER 25 **Nobody's Home**

Have you ever known someone who wanted "more of the same" in a way that
only made them feel lonely? Have you ever been that person?

Have you ever craved more of something even if possessing it would harm
those around you?

Dorothy rejoices when Toto runs away, leaving her more alone than ever.

Have you ever known such a moment?

CHAPTER 26 **On a Mission**

When have you brought too much stuff on a mission?

When have you been in a community where gifts emerged right when they
were needed?

Have gifts you never knew you had emerged right when they were most needed?

CHAPTER 27 **Not So Fast**

Has your life had its missions? When were there times when you were sent to
accomplish an important task?

Who were your companions? What gifts did they have or lack?

When have you had to rely on others who weren't always sure of themselves?

Recall a time you had to go up against long odds feeling that you lacked something essential. What was that like?

Have you had to move through disappointment and defeat, only to move on to
the next chapter of your life?

CHAPTER 28 **Confirmation**

People "sometimes need help seeing in themselves qualities that are
easily recognized by those around them." Has that ever been true of you?

Have you been becoming something slowly, day by day, with the help of those
around you? What are you becoming?

A sacramental is "an outward, visible sign; a token, of the inner,
invisible reality." What's the most important one you've received?

What do you think about The Wizard's statement, "a heart is not judged by how much you love, but by how much you are loved by others?"

CHAPTER 29 **Into Thin Air**

Have you ever been in an atmosphere with lots of energy and little real substance?

Have you ever, like Dorothy, wanted something so badly that you believed in it, even when you knew it wasn't real?

Have you ever, like The Wizard, let another believe you could do something that you knew you could not?

CHAPTER 30 **Sterile**

Did you ever receive a kind offer to settle for less than a goal you felt you needed to pursue?

Have you ever chosen to live a part of your life closed off to new relationships?

Have you ever chosen to risk your heart, even if it might hurt?

Are you good at asking yourself, "What have I learned?"

CHAPTER 31 **No Place Like Home**

Do you have a meditative practice — or anything like it — that helps you move into your heart of hearts?

Does this scene make you think of anything similar in your life? Have you ever awakened in a way that was hard to make others understand?

Have you ever had a profound experience of coming home?

EPILOGUE: **The End And A New Beginning**

When did you begin to say, "I love you?"

How are the words, "I love you" spoken in your family and in your circle of friends?

"Those she'd said a tearful goodbye to were given back to her, only slightly different, in the next scene." Do you think we'll ultimately be given back to those we love?

About Good Dog Outreach

Good Dog Outreach, publishers of *And Toto, Too: The Wizard of Oz as a Spiritual Adventure*, is a nonprofit organization dedicated to the total transformation of human consciousness – and nothing less.

We want everyone, everywhere, to be happy.
We specialize in creating books and retreats and workshops that help encourage everyone to be Young in Heart.

To learn more, visit www.andtoto.org